VISUAL QUICKSTART GUIDE

InDesign

FOR MACINTOSH AND WINDOWS

Sandee Cohen

D1308446

Peachpit Press

Visual QuickStart Guide
InDesign for Macintosh and Windows
Copyright © 1999 by Sandee Cohen

Peachpit Press
1249 Eighth Street
Berkeley, CA 94710
800 283-9444 • 510 524 2178
fax 510 524 2221
Find us on the Web at http://www.peachpit.com

Peachpit Press is a division of Addison Wesley Longman

Development Editor: Nancy Davis
Copy Editor: Nancy Dunn
Production Coordinator: Kate Reber
Compositor & Interior Design: Sandee Cohen
Cover Design: The Visual Group
Indexer: Steve Rath

ISBN 0-201-35447-0

0 9 8 7 6 5 4 3 2 1

Printed and bound in the United States of America

DEDICATED TO

My family

THANKS TO

Nancy Ruenzel, publisher of Peachpit Press.

Nancy Davis, my project editor at Peachpit Press. You made this project far less daunting.

Nancy Dunn, who is more than a copy editor; she is a great friend.

Kate Reber of Peachpit Press, who does a great job of production.

The staff of Peachpit Press, all of whom make me proud to be a Peachpit author.

Steve Rath, who does the best index in the business.

Tim Cole of Adobe, who was a great source of information and an exceptional dinner companion.

Jean-Claude Tremblay of the InDesign beta list. His advice was so terrific it took me a while to realize he was another beta tester and doesn't work for Adobe. I can't think of anyone who knows more about desktop publishing than Jean-Claude.

InDesign beta testers, too numerous to name, who all contributed insight, tips, and techniques as we all tried to climb this new K2 mountain.

Robert Ransick and the staff of the New School for Social Research Computer Instruction Center.

Pixel, my cat, who has gotten very blasé about these books and doesn't watch me work anymore.

Colophon

This book was created using QuarkXPress 4 for layout and Ambrosia SW Snapz Pro for screen shots. The computers used were a Power Macintosh™ 8500 and a PowerBook G3. InDesign for Windows 98 ran on the Macintosh platform using Virtual PC 2.1.1. The fonts used were Minion and Futura from Adobe and two specialty fonts created using Macromedia Fontographer. Some images are copyright by www.arttoday.com. Witch photograph from the KPT Power Photos collections.

TABLE OF CONTENTS

INTRODUCTION

Welcome to Adobe InDesign. Rarely has the introduction of an application caused as much excitement as this one. For the past several years, desktop publishing insiders have heard whispers and rumors about InDesign—first under the code-name K2, and then as InDesign. In March, 1999, the program had a preview release at Seybold Seminars in Boston. Now, after over five years of active development (and over fifteen years of experience in desktop publishing), Adobe Systems Inc. has released InDesign.

InDesign has some very revolutionary features. It uses new plug-in technology that allows the program to be a series of different plug-ins. This means that InDesign can be updated and modified extremely easily. InDesign also has some of the most powerful typography technology that has ever been in a consumer desktop publishing application.

Of course, the major question is "Is InDesign a Quark killer?" referring to how InDesign compares to QuarkXPress. The answer to that question remains to be seen and is outside the scope of this book.

I created this book as a teaching tool—a QuickStart Guide to help you understand and use InDesign. As you become familiar with the program, you can answer the question yourself.

Using This Book

If you have used any of the Visual QuickStart Guides, you will find this book to be similar. Each of the chapters consists of numbered steps that deal with a specific technique or feature of the program. As you work through the steps, you gain an understanding of the technique or feature. The illustrations help you judge if you are following the steps correctly.

Instructions

You will find it easier to use this book once you understand the terms I am using. This is especially important since some other computer books use terms differently. Therefore, here are the terms I use in the book and explanations of what they mean.

Click refers to pressing down and releasing the mouse button on the Macintosh, or the left mouse button on Windows. You must release the mouse button or it is not a click.

Press means to hold down the mouse button, or a keyboard key.

Press and drag means to hold the mouse button down and then move the mouse. I also use the shorthand term *drag*. Just remember that you have to press and hold as you drag the mouse.

Menu Commands

InDesign has menu commands that you follow to open dialog boxes, change artwork, and initiate certain actions. These menu commands are listed in bold type. The typical direction to choose a menu command might be written as **Object > Arrange > Bring to Front**. This means that you should first choose the Object menu, then choose the Arrange submenu, and then choose the Bring to Front command.

Keyboard Shortcuts

Most of the menu commands for InDesign have keyboard shortcuts that help you work faster. For instance, instead of choosing New from the File menu, it is faster and easier to use the keyboard shortcut (Command-N on the Macintosh and Ctrl-N on Windows).

The modifier keys used in keyboard shortcuts are sometimes listed in different orders by different software companies or authors. For example, I always list the Command or Ctrl keys first, then the Option or Alt key, and then the Shift key. Other people may list the Shift key first. The order that you press those modifier keys is not important. However, it is very important that you always add the last key (the letter or number key) after you are pressing the other keys.

You might expect that this book would list all the keyboard shortcuts for InDesign. There are two reasons why I haven't done that. First, InDesign lets you assign your own keyboard shortcuts. So I don't know which keyboard shortcuts you're going to use. Second, you can easily create a list of all the shortcuts in InDesign and print them out yourself. So although you would be impressed if I provided a list of keyboard shortcuts, see Chapter 14 for how you can create them yourself.

Learning Keyboard Shortcuts

While keyboard shortcuts help you work faster, you really do not have to start using them right away. In fact, you will most likely learn more about InDesign by using the menus. As you look for one command, you may see another feature that you would like to explore.

Once you feel comfortable working with InDesign, you can start adding keyboard shortcuts to your repertoire. My suggestion is to look at which menu commands you use a lot. Then each day choose one of those shortcuts. For instance, if you import a lot of art from other programs, you might decide to learn the shortcut for the Place command. For the rest of that day use the Import shortcut every time you import art. Even if you have to look at the menu to refresh your memory, still use the keyboard shortcut to actually open the Import dialog box. By the end of the day you will have memorized the Place shortcut. The next day you can learn a new one.

Cross-Platform Issues

One of the great strengths of InDesign is that it is almost identical on both the Macintosh and Windows platforms. In fact, at first glance it is hard to tell which platform you are working on. However, because there are some differences between the platforms, there are some things you should keep in mind.

Modifier Keys

Modifier keys are always listed with the Macintosh key first and then the Windows key second. So the direction "Hold the Command/Ctrl key" means hold the Command key on the Macintosh platform or the Ctrl key on the Windows platform. When the key is the same on both computers, such as the Shift key, only one key is listed.

Generally the Command key on the Macintosh (sometimes called the Apple key) corresponds to the Ctrl key on Windows. The Option key on the Macintosh corresponds to the Alt key on Windows. The Control key on the Macintosh does not have an equivalent on Windows. Notice that the Control key for the Macintosh is always spelled out while the Ctrl key for Windows is not.

Platform-Specific Features

A few times in the book, I have written separate exercises for the Macintosh and Windows platforms. These exercises are indicated by (Mac) and (Win).

Most of the time this is because the procedures are so different that they need to be written separately. Some features exist only on one platform. Those features are then labeled as to their platform.

Coming from other programs

It is very likely that some users of InDesign are experts in other page layout programs. If you are familiar with other programs, you should look at Chapters 15 and 16 which compare InDesign features to those in QuarkXPress or PageMaker.

Updates and Fixes on the Web

One of the advantages to InDesign is that it is very modular. This means that Adobe will be able to post updates and changes to InDesign on the Adobe Web site. Similarly, I will be able to post updates, changes, and additional tips on the Peachpit Web site. Just go to www.peachpit.com and look up the *InDesign for Macintosh and Windows: Visual QuickStart Guide.* I'll be posting information on the book's companion Web pages.

Just remember to have fun!

Sandee Cohen

(SandeeC@aol.com)
September, 1999

GETTING STARTED 1

When I start learning a new application, I'm always in a rush to get started. When I pick up a book about the application, I never read the first chapter.

I don't want to read about buttons, fields, and controls — especially if I'm already familiar with other programs from the company, such as Photoshop and Illustrator.

I rush right into the middle chapters of the book.

However, after a few hours of slogging helplessly through the book, I realize there are things I don't understand about the program. I realize I'm a bit confused. So I come back to the first chapter to learn the foundation of the program.

Of course, since you're much more patient than I am, you're already here — reading the first chapter.

Using Palettes

Most of the commands and features in
InDesign are found in the 19 onscreen
palettes. Each of these palettes covers
special features. These palettes are very
similar to those found in other Adobe
applications.

Align Palette

The Align palette ❶ aligns and distributes
objects on a page *(see Chapter 4, "Working
with Objects")*.

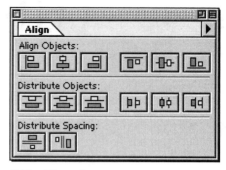

❶ The Align palette.

Attributes Palette

The Attributes palette ❷ allows you to set
fills and strokes to overprint *(see Chapter 6,
"Working in Color")*.

❷ The Attributes palette.

Character Palette

The Character palette ❸ controls character-
level attributes such as the typeface and
point size *(see Chapter 3, "Text")*.

Character Styles Palette

The Character Styles palette ❹ lets you
define and work with character styles *(see
Chapter 9, "Automating Text")*.

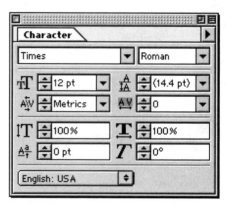

❸ The Character palette.

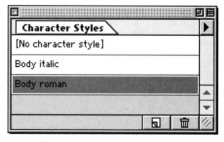

❹ The Character Styles palette.

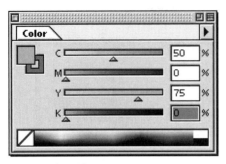

⑤ The Color palette.

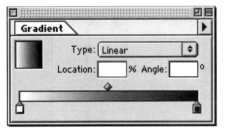

⑥ The Gradient palette.

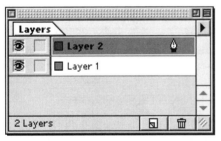

⑦ The Layers palette.

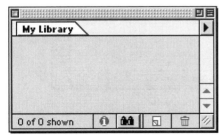

⑧ The Library palette.

Color Palette

The Color palette **⑤** allows you to mix or apply colors *(see Chapter 6, "Working in Color")*.

Gradient Palette

The Gradient palette **⑥** controls the appearance of gradients *(see Chapter 6, "Working in Color")*.

Layers Palette

The Layers palette **⑦** controls the stacking order of different layers *(see Chapter 8, "Long Documents")*.

Library Palette

The Library palette **⑧** lets you store and use elements *(see Chapter 8, "Long Documents")*.

Using Palettes

Links Palette

The Links palette **9** controls the status of placed images *(see Chapter 7, "Imported Graphics")*.

Navigator Palette

The Navigator palette **10** lets you see the layout of pages *(see Chapter 2, "Document Setup")*.

Pages Palette

The Pages palette **11** lets you add and control pages *(see Chapter 8, "Long Documents")*.

9 The Links palette.

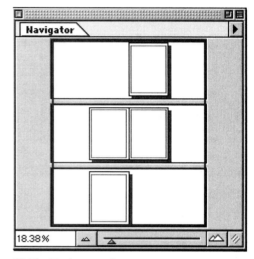

10 The Navigator palette.

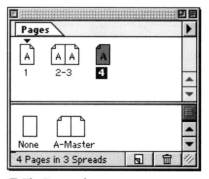

11 The Pages palette.

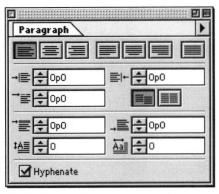

⑫ The Paragraph palette.

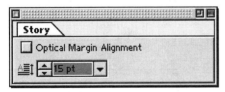

⑬ The Paragraph Styles palette.

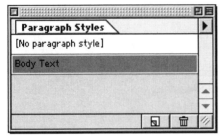

⑭ The Story palette.

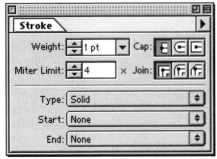

⑮ The Stroke palette.

Paragraph Palette

The Pagraph palette **⑫** controls paragraph-level attributes such as the alignment and margin indents *(see Chapter 3, "Text")*.

Paragraph Styles Palette

The Paragraph Styles palette **⑬** lets you define and work with character styles *(see Chapter 9, "Automating Text")*.

Story Palette

The Story palette **⑭** controls the optical margin alignment *(see Chapter 10, "Advanced Text")*.

Stroke Palette

The Stroke palette **⑮** controls the stroke attributes *(see Chapter 4, "Working with Objects")*.

Using Palettes

Swatches Palette

The Swatches palette ⑯ stores the colors in a document *(see Chapter 6, "Working in Color").*

Tabs Palette

The Tabs palette ⑰ controls the position of the tab stops for text *(see Chapter 9, "Automating Text").*

Text Wrap Palette

The Text Wrap palette ⑱ controls how text wraps around objects *(see Chapter 10, "Advanced Text").*

Transform Palette

The Transform palette ⑲ controls the size and position of objects *(see Chapter 4, "Working with Objects").*

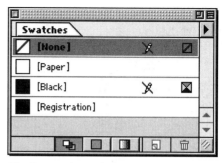

⑯ The Swatches palette.

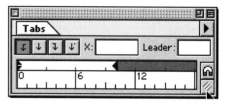

⑰ The Tabs palette.

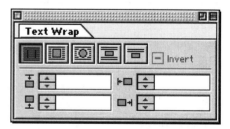

⑱ The Text Wrap palette.

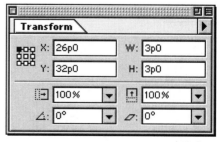

⑲ The Transform palette.

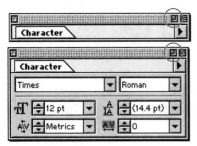

㉑ Click the **Resize button** to expand or collapse a palette.

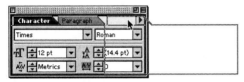

㉑ Drag the **palette tab** to nest palettes.

Working with Palettes

There are some special features you can use when working with palettes.

Resize button

Click the resize button **㉑** to expand and collapse a palette.

Tabs

Drag the palette tab **㉑** to nest one palette with another or to separate nested palettes.

Working with Interface Elements

Each of the dialog boxes and palettes has various interface elements to control the features. These are very similar to interface elements found in other applications.

Buttons

Click to activate a button ㉒.

Checkboxes

Click to activate a checkbox ㉓.

Fields

Highlight the value and type a new number in a field ㉔.

Field Controls

Click the up or down arrows next to a field ㉕ to increase or decrease the values.

Icons

Click to choose an icon ㉖.

Pop-up Lists

Click to choose the items in a pop-up list ㉗.

Radio buttons

Click to apply a radio button ㉘.

Sliders

Drag a slider to increase or decrease the value in a field ㉙.

Submenus

Click to display the submenu at the side of a palette ㉚. Click again to choose an item in a submenu.

㉒ Click to activate a **button.**

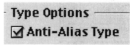

㉓ Click to activate a checkbox.

㉔ Enter values in a **field.**

㉕ Click the **field controls** to increase or decrease the values.

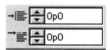

㉖ Click to choose an **icon.**

㉗ Click to choose the items in a a a **pop-up list.**

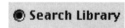

㉘ Click to select a **radio button.**

㉙ Drag to change the values of a **slider.**

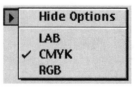

㉚ Click to choose the items in a submenu.

Working with Interface Elements

Using the Toolbox

The Toolbox contains 20 different tools as well as controls for the color controls of fills and strokes ❸❶. Some of the tools have fly-out controls that let you access the other tools in the category.

To choose a tool:

◆ Click the tool in the Toolbox.

or

Tap the keyboard command.

To choose a fly-out tool:

◆ Press and choose a tool.

or

Hold the Shift key and tap the keyboard command

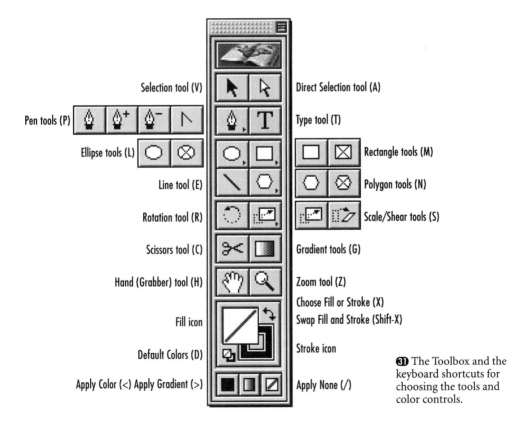

Selection tool (V)

Direct Selection tool (A)

Pen tools (P)

Type tool (T)

Ellipse tools (L)

Rectangle tools (M)

Line tool (E)

Polygon tools (N)

Rotation tool (R)

Scale/Shear tools (S)

Scissors tool (C)

Gradient tools (G)

Hand (Grabber) tool (H)

Zoom tool (Z)

Choose Fill or Stroke (X)

Fill icon

Swap Fill and Stroke (Shift-X)

Stroke icon

Default Colors (D)

Apply Color (<) Apply Gradient (>)

Apply None (/)

❸❶ The Toolbox and the keyboard shortcuts for choosing the tools and color controls.

To choose Fill or Stroke:

◆ Click the Fill or Stroke icon in the Toolbox.

or

Tap X on the keyboard.

32 The Swap **Fill and Stroke** icon in the Toolbox.

To swap the Fill or Stroke settings:

◆ Click the Swap Fill or Stroke icon **32** in the Toolbox.

or

Tap Shift-X on the keyboard.

33 The **Apply Color icon** in the Toolbox.

To apply the current color:

◆ Click the Apply Color icon **33** in the Toolbox.

or

Tap < on the keyboard.

34 The **Apply Gradient icon** in the Toolbox.

To apply the current gradient:

◆ Click the Apply Gradient icon **34** in the Toolbox.

or

Tap > on the keyboard.

35 The **Apply None icon** in the Toolbox.

To apply no color:

◆ Click the Apply None icon **35** in the Toolbox.

or

Tap / on the keyboard.

Over selected object

Over Ruler

Over Page

36 Examples of some of the **Contextual menus** in InDesign.

Using Contextual Menus

Contextual menus are menus that change depending on the type of object selected or where the mouse is positioned **36**.

To Display Contextual Menus:

◆ (Mac) Hold the Control key and click the mouse button.

or

(Win) Click the right mouse button.

Using Contextual Menus

DOCUMENT SETUP 2

Billions of years ago, when dinosaurs ruled the earth, (or just fifteen years ago, before the beginning of desktop publishing), people prepared documents for printing by creating pieces of stiff board. They marked up the boards with special nonprinting blue pencils to indicate the edges of the pages. They drew marks that indicated where the margins and columns should be and how to trim the pages. This board, or *mechanical,* was then used as the layout for the document.

Unlike the board mechanicals of the past, InDesign documents are electronic layouts. Just as with the board mechanicals, you need to set the page sizes, margins, and column widths. However, since you are using a computer, there are additional controls for how the document is viewed.

It helps enormously if you know most of the details about the document setup before you begin work. For instance, you might find out in the middle of a project that the margins are too wide to hold all the text. While you can always change the margins later, it helps if you have an idea of what size they should be before you do too much work. Of course, all changes to your electronic layout take far less time than they did on board mechanicals.

Starting Documents

When you create a new document, you have to answer a lot of questions. This is the same as marking up a mechanical board.

To start a new document:

1. Choose **File >New.** This opens the Document Setup dialog box **❶**.

2. Type the number of pages in the Number of Pages field.

3. Check Facing Pages to set your document with left-hand and right-hand pages. *(See the next page for more information on facing pages.)*

4. Check Master Text Frame to automatically add text to pages. *(For more information on master text frames, see page 140.)*

5. Use the Page Size pop-up list to set the size of your page. *(See the next page.)*

6. Set the Orientation to portrait or landscape. *(For more information on the page orientation, see page 20.)*

7. Enter the size of the margins in the Margins fields. *(For more information on setting the margins, see page 24.)*

8. Set the number of columns and the gutter width in the Columns Number and Gutter fields. *(For more information on columns and gutters, see page 21.)*

9. Click OK. The document appears in the window **❷**.

TIP The pages are surrounded by an area called the pasteboard. Items on the pasteboard do not print.

To open previously saved documents:

1. Choose **File >Open.**

2. Navigate through your directories and folders to find the file you want to open.

3. Click OK.

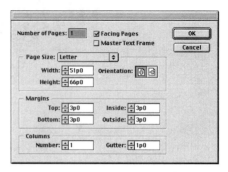

❶ The **Document Setup** dialog box offers basic layout options.

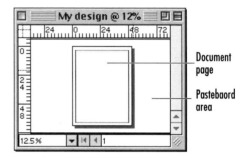

❷ Each document page is surrounded by the pasteboard area where you can temporarily store objects for use later.

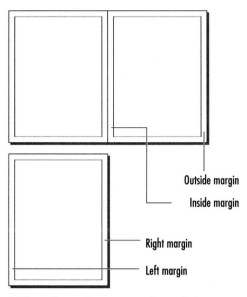

Outside margin

Inside margin

Right margin

Left margin

❸ The difference between margins on **facing pages** (top) and **nonfacing pages** (bottom).

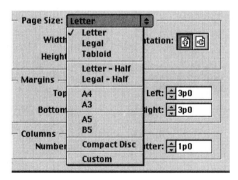

❹ The **Page Size** pop-up list offers standard U.S. and international paper sizes, as well as customization controls.

Choosing Layout Options

The term *facing pages* refers to documents such as books where pages on one side of a spine face the pages on the other side. (This is also called a *spread.*) Single pages, such as advertisements, are set with facing pages turned off.

To set facing pages:

◆ With the Document Setup dialog box open, click Facing Pages. This gives you left- and right-hand pages in your document ❸.

TIP When a document is set for facing pages, the left and right margins change to inside and outside margins.

The page size is the size of the individual pages of the document.

To set the size of the page:

◆ Press the pop-up list ❹ to choose the page size. The 11 choices are as follows:

- Letter, 8 1/2 by 11 inches.
- Legal, 8 1/2 by 14 inches.
- Tabloid, 11 by 17 inches.
- Letter–Half, 8 1/2 by 5 1/2 inches.
- Legal–Half, 8 1/2 by 7 inches.
- A4, 21 by 29.7 centimeters.
- A3, 29.7 by 42 centimeters.
- A5, 14.8 by 21 centimeters.
- B5, 17.6 by 25 centimeters.
- Compact Disc, 4.7222 by 4.75 inches.
- Custom, which allows you to enter your own specific values.

TIP The A4, A3, A5, and B5 sizes are used primarily outside of the United States.

TIP If you change the values in the Width or the Height fields, the Page Size automatically switches to the Custom setting.

The term *orientation* refers to how the page is positioned, either up and down or sideways.

To set the orientation:

◆ Click the Portrait orientation ❺ to create a document where the width is always less than the height.

or

Click the Landscape orientation ❺ to create a document where the width is always greater than the height.

To set the margins:

1. Click the field controls or enter an amount for the Top and Bottom fields.

2. If the document is set for facing pages, click the field controls or enter an amount for the Inside and Outside fields ❻.

or

If the document is not set for facing pages, click the field controls or enter an amount for the Left and Right margins ❼.

To set the columns and gutters:

1. Click the field controls or enter an amount for the number of columns.

2. Click the field controls or enter an amount for the *gutter,* or the space between the columns.

TIP The columns and gutters act as guidelines on your page ❽. You can still place text or graphics across the columns or gutters.

To set the document defaults:

◆ Change the document setup or any of the other attributes with no page open, to set the defaults for all new pages.

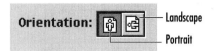

❺ The **orientation** choices let you set the position of the page.

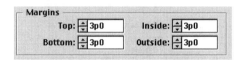

❻ The **margin settings** for a document with facing pages.

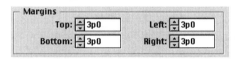

❼ The **margin settings** for a document with non-facing pages.

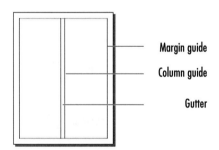

❽ A document with margin and column guides.

⊙ The **Document Setup** dialog box for an existing document.

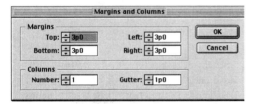

⑩ The **Margins and Columns** dialog box for an existing document.

Changing Layout Options

You may discover that you need to change some of the settings of a document. Although all the settings appear in one dialog box to start a new document, there are two separate controls to make changes to the document.

To change the document setup:

1. Choose **File** > **Document Setup** to open the Document Setup dialog box **⊙**.

2. Make whatever changes you want to the following settings:

   - Number of Pages

   - Facing Pages

   - Page Size

   - Orientation

3. Click OK to apply the changes to the document.

To change the margins and columns:

1. Choose **Layout** > **Margins and Columns** to open the Margins and Columns dialog box **⑩**.

2. Make whatever changes you want to the following settings:

   - Margins.

   - Number of columns.

   - Gutter or the width of the space between the columns.

3. Click OK to apply the changes to the document.

TIP Changing the margins and columns while on a page or spread changes the settings only for that page or spread. To change the settings for all the pages, you need to work with the Master Page. *(For more information on master pages, see Chapter 8, "Long Documents.")*

Using Document Rulers

Just as you use a ruler to measure a mechanical, InDesign gives you electronic rulers you can customize or hide.

To show and hide the document rulers:

◆ To see the rulers along the top and left edges of the document window **⓫**, choose View>Show Rulers.

or

To hide the rulers, choose View>Hide Rulers.

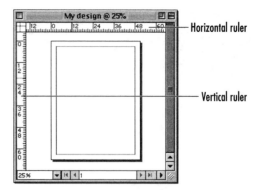

⓫ The horizontal and vertical rulers.

You can change the rulers to different units of measurement. This is especially helpful if you receive instructions written in measurements with which you are not familiar.

To change the unit of measurement:

1. Choose File>Preferences>Units and Increments. This opens the Units and Increments dialog box.

2. For the Horizontal and Vertical settings, choose one of the measurements from the pop-up lists **⓬**.

3. If you choose the Custom setting, enter the number of points for each unit on the ruler.

TIP You can use the Custom setting to create a vertical ruler that corresponds to the document's leading so that each unit equals each line of copy.

TIP You can change the unit of measurements with the ruler contextual menus **⓭**. *(See page 15 for information on how to access contextual menus.)*

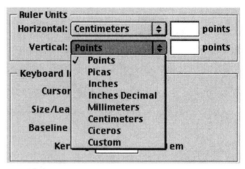

⓬ The choices for the rulers **units of measurement**.

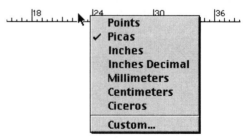

⓭ The ruler contextual menu.

Using Document Ruler

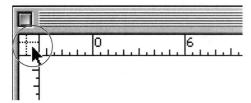

14 The **zero point indicator** of the rulers.

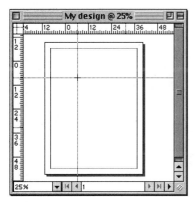

15 You set the ruler's zero point bgy dragging the zero point indicator to a new position on the page.

The rulers start numbering at the top-left corner of the page. You may want to move this point, called a *zero point,* to a different position. This might help you judge how much space you have from one spot of the page to another.

To reposition the zero point:

1. Position the cursor over the zero point crosshairs at the upper-left corner of the rulers **14**.

2. Drag the zero point to the new position on the page **15**.

3. Release the mouse button to position the zero point.

TIP Double-click the zero point crosshairs in the corner of the rulers to reset the zero point to the upper-left corner.

Setting Margin and Column Guides

Guides are nonprinting lines that help you position text and graphics on the page. InDesign has different types of guides: Margin guides can be used to indicate where elements, such as page numbers, belong. Column guides can be used to divide text from graphics ⑯.

To show and hide guides:

◆ To see the margin, column, and ruler guides, choose **View>Show Guides**.

or

To hide the guides, choose **View>Hide Guides**.

TIP The Show Guides command also displays the ruler guides *(see the following page)*.

If you have not changed the default settings, InDesign displays the margin guides in pink, the column guides in blue. You may want to change those colors, especially if you have objects on the page that use similar colors.

To change the appearance of margin and column guides:

1. Choose **File>Preferences>Guides** to open the Guides Preferences dialog box ⑰.

2. Use the Margins pop-up list to set the color of the margin guides.

3. Use the Columns pop-up list to set the color of the column guides.

4. Check Guides in Back to position the guides behind text and graphics on the page ⑱.

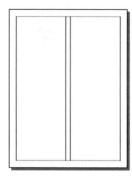

⑯ A sample page with **margin guides and column guides**.

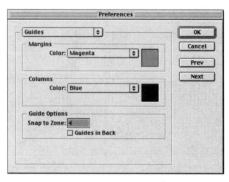

⑰ The dialog box for the **guides preferences**.

Guides in Back turned on

Guides in Back turned off

⑱ The effect of turning off **Guides in Back**.

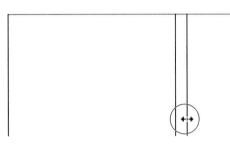

19 The **two-headed arrow** indicates that a column guide can be moved.

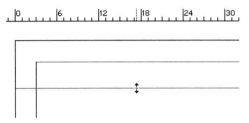

20 You can drag **ruler guides** out from the horizontal ruler or vertical ruler.

There may be times when you want to move the column guides manually. This gives you a custom guide setting.

To move column guides:

1. Position the cursor over the guide you want to move.

2. Press the mouse button. The cursor turns into a two-headed arrow **19** that indicates that the column has been selected.

3. Drag the column guide to the new position.

TIP You cannot change the width of the gutter space between the columns by moving a column guide.

Using Ruler Guides

Another type of guide is the ruler guide. Ruler guides are more flexible than margin or column guides and can be positioned anywhere on the page. You create individual ruler guides by pulling a guide out from the ruler.

To pull a guide from the ruler:

1. Position the cursor over the horizontal or vertical ruler. *(To display the rulers, see page 22.)*

2. Press the mouse button. The cursor turns into a two-headed arrow.

2. Drag to pull the guide out onto the page **20**.

Rather than pulling guides out one at a time, you can also create a series of ruler guides in rows and columns.

To create rows and columns using guides:

1. Choose **Layout** > **Create Guides**. This opens the Create Guides dialog box **㉑**.

2. Type the number of rows (horizontal guides) in the Rows Number field.

3. Type the amount for the space between the rows in the Rows Gutter field.

4. Type the number of columns (vertical guides) in the Columns Number field.

5. Type the amount for the space between the columns in the Columns Gutter field.

6. Choose between Fit Guides to Margins or Page **㉒**.

7. Check Remove Existing Guides to delete all ruler guides previously on the page.

8. Click OK to apply the guides.

TIP Check Preview to see the page change as you enter the values within the dialog box.

To reposition ruler guides:

1. Position the cursor over the guide you want to move.

2. Press the mouse button. The cursor turns into a two-headed arrow and the guide changes to a darker color. This indicates that the guide has been selected.

3. Drag the ruler guide to a new position.

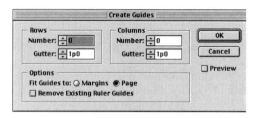

㉑ The **Create Guides** dialog box.

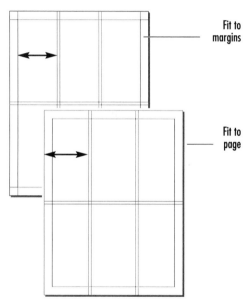

Fit to margins

Fit to page

㉒ The difference between **Fit Guides to Margin** and **Fit Guides to Page**. Notice the difference between the position of the guides.

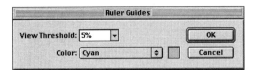

❷❸ You can change the Ruler Guides color in the **Ruler Guides** dialog box. You can also set at what magnification the guides should be seen.

❷❹ Setting the view threshold to 200% means that the guides are visible only when the magnification is 200% or higher.

Just as you can change margin guides, you can change the color of ruler guides. In addition to the guide color, you can also set the view threshold. This is the magnification at which the guides are not visible.

To change the appearance of ruler guides:

1. Choose **Layout > Ruler Guides** to open the dialog box **❷❸**.

2. Use the Color pop-up list to pick the color for the ruler guides.

3. Set a percentage for the View Threshold in the field. This sets the amount of magnification below which the ruler guides are not displayed **❷❹**.

TIP Increase the View Threshold if you have many guides on the page. This hides the guides at low magnifications and shows them at higher ones. *(See page 29 for more information on setting the view magnifications.)*

You may want to lock your guides so they don't move inadvertently.

To lock guides:

◆ Choose **View > Lock Guides.**

TIP Choose the command again to unlock the guides.

Objects can be set to snap to guides. This makes it easier to align objects to guides.

To turn on Snap to Guides:

◆ Choose **View > Snap to Guides.**

To change the snap-to distance:

1. Choose **File > Preferences > Guides.**

2. Enter an amount in the Snap to Zone. This is how close to a guide (in pixels) an object must be before it snaps to the guide.

Ruler Guides

Working With Document Grids

The document grid lets you fill the page with lines to which you can align objects. The baseline grid ensures that different text lines up horizontally. *(See page 53 for how to work with the baseline grid.)*

To display the grids:

◆ Choose View>Show Document Grid or View>Show Baseline Grid.

To hide the grids:

◆ Choose View>Hide Document Grid or View>Hide Baseline Grid.

To change the grid apperance:

1. Choose File>Preferences>Grid. This opens the Grid Preferences dialog box ㉕.

2. Use the Color pop-up list to change the grid color.

3. Enter an amount in the Gridline Every field to set the distance between the main gridlines.

4. Enter an amount in the Subdivisions field to create lighter gridlines between the main gridlines.

5. Enter an amount in Baseline Grid Start field to set where the baseline grid should start on the page.

6. Enter an percentage in the Baseline Grid View Threshold field. This sets the lowest magnification that the grid is visible at.

To turn on Snap to Grid:

◆ Choose View>Snap to Document Grid. If Snap to Document Grid is checked, the feature is already turned on.

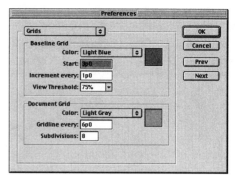

㉕ The **Grids Preferences** dialog box.

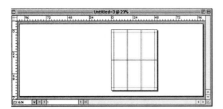

26 The **Fit Entire Pasteboard** command shows the page as well as the pasteboard.

Changing the Magnification

Magnification refers to the size of the document as it appears on your screen. InDesign gives you a many ways to change the magnification setting. Some of the quickest and easiest ways to change the magnification settings are to use view commands.

TIP Because the View commands are used so often, the keyboard shortcuts are listed here. You can also find those shortcuts listed on the View menu.

To zoom with the view commands:

1. To increase the magnification, choose **View>Zoom In.**

   Shortcut: Command/Ctrl-+.

2. To decrease the magnification, choose **View>Zoom Out.**

   Shortcut: Command/Ctrl-– (hyphen).

3. To see all of the current page, choose **View>Fit Page In Window.** This changes the magnification setting to whatever amount is necessary to see the entire page.

   Shortcut: Command/Ctrl-0 (zero).

TIP Small monitors force you to use small magnifications to see the entire page. Larger monitors show the entire page at magnifications that are easier to read.

4. To see all of the current spread, choose **View>Fit Spread In Window.** *(See page 19 for more information on working with spreads)*

   Shortcut: Command-Opt-0 (Mac) or Ctrl-Alt-0 (Win).

5. To see the document at a 100% magnification, choose **View>Actual Size.**

   Shortcut: Command/Ctrl-1.

6. To see the entire pasteboard area **26**, choose **View>Fit Entire Pasteboard.**

Changing the Magnification

You can set the page to a specific magnification amount by selecting from the magnification list.

To use the magnification list:

1. Click the control at the bottom-left corner of the window to display the magnification list 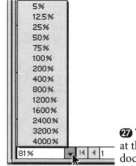.

2. Choose one of the magnifications in the list.

27 The **magnification list** at the bottom of the document window.

You can also view specific magnifications not in the list.

To enter a specific magnification amount :

1. Double-click or drag across the magnification shown.

2. Type a number between 5 and 4000.

TIP It is not necessary to type the % sign.

3. Press Return or Enter to apply the setting.

Changing the Magnification

㉘ The **Zoom tool** in the Toolbox.

Using the Zoom and Hand Tools

The Zoom tool lets you jump to a specific magnification and position on the page. The Hand tool moves the view to a new position.

To use the Zoom tool:

1. Click the Zoom tool in the Toolbox **㉘**. The cursor turns into a magnifying glass.

2. Click the Zoom tool on the area you want to zoom in on. Click as many times as is necessary to change the magnification.

TIP Press Command/Ctrl and Spacebar to access the Zoom tool without leaving the tool that is currently selected.

TIP Each click of the Zoom tool changes the magnification to the next setting in the magnification list.

TIP Press the Option/Alt key while in the Zoom tool to zoom out. The icon changes from a plus sign (+) to a minus sign (–).

TIP Double-click the Zoom tool in the Toolbox to set the view to the actual size (100%).

A *marquee zoom* allows you to zoom quickly to a certain magnification and position.

To create a marquee zoom:

♦ Drag the Zoom tool diagonally across the area you want to see. Release the mouse button to zoom in **㉙ – ㉚**.

㉙ Drag the Zoom tool to magnify a specific area. The dotted line indicates the area to be selected.

㉚ The selected area fills the window after you release the mouse button.

You can also use the Hand tool (sometimes called the *Grabber* tool) to move around within the area of the document. This is more flexible than using the scrollbars.

To use the Hand tool:

1. Click the Hand tool in the Toolbox **31**.

2. Drag the Hand tool to move around the page.

TIP Hold the Spacebar to access the Hand tool without leaving the tool currently selected.

TIP To access the Hand tool while in a text block, hold the Opt/Alt key as you press the mouse button.

TIP Double-click the Hand tool in the Toolbox to fit the entire page in the window.

31 Click the **Hand tool** in the Toolbox to move the page around the window.

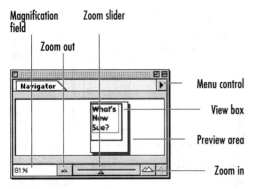

Magnification field
Zoom slider
Zoom out
Menu control
View box
Preview area
Zoom in

② The Navigator palette.

Using the Navigator Palette

The Navigator palette combines the functions of both the Zoom and Hand tools.

To use the Navigator zoom buttons:

1. If the Navigator palette is not open, choose **Window>Navigator.** This opens the Navigator palette **②**.

2. Click the Zoom In button to increase the magnification.

3. Click the Zoom Out button to decrease the magnification.

To set a specific magnification:

1. Highlight the value in the Magnification Amount field and enter the specific magnification value.

2. Press Return or Enter to apply the magnification.

The Zoom slider lets you increase or decrease the magnification.

To use the Zoom slider:

◆ Drag the Zoom slider to the right to increase the magnification.

or

Drag the slider to the left to decrease the magnification.

TIP The Preview Box shows the area that will be displayed at each position of the slider.

Using the Navigator Palette

The Preview Box within the Navigator palette can also be used to move around the page.

To move using the Preview Box:

1. Position the cursor inside the Preview Area of the Navigator palette. The cursor changes into a hand **33**.

2. Drag the Hand around the Preview Area. The Preview Box moves to change the area displayed within the document window.

TIP Choose Navigator Options from the Navigator menu to change the color of the Preview Box.

TIP In a multipage document, choose View Active Spread from the Navigator palette menu to see only the active spread rather than all the pages of the document. *(See Chapter 8, "Long Documents" for working with multipage documents.)*

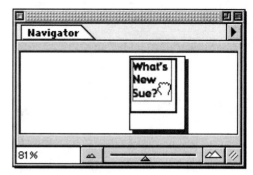

33 The **Hand cursor** inside the Preview Area.

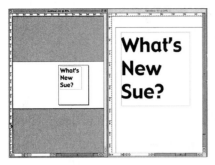

34 Two views of the same document set to tiled.

Controlling Windows

InDesign window commands let you view one document in two windows and control the display of multiple windows.

To see a document in two windows:

1. Choose **Window>New Window.** This creates a second window containing the document.

2. Choose **Window>Tile.** This changes the size of the two windows and positions them side by side on your screen **34**.

   or

   Choose **Window>Cascade.** This stacks all the open windows so that their title bars are visible.

Saving Documents

After you work on a document for a while, you must save your work as a file to a hard drive or disk. This is vital so that you don't lose important information should your computer crash.

To save and name a file (Win):

1. Choose **File** > **Save** or **File** > **Save As.** This opens the Save As dialog box **35**.

2. Use the Save In field to choose a destination disk and folder for the file.

3. Use the File Name field to name the file.

4. Use the Save As Type field to choose between an InDesign document or an InDesign Template.

TIP The template format saves the file so that each time it is opened, it opens as an untitled document. This protects the document from inadvertant changes.

5. Click Save to save the file and close the dialog box.

To save and name a file (Mac):

1. Choose **File** > **Save** or **File** > **Save As.** This opens the Save As dialog box **36**.

2. Use the Macintosh navigational elements to choose a destination disk and folder for the file.

3. Use the Name field to name the file.

4. Use the Format pop-up list to choose between an InDesign document or the stationery option.

5. If you choose Stationery Option, click Stationery in the Stationery Option dialog box **37**.

TIP The Stationery format saves the file so that each time it is opened, it opens as an untitled document. This protects the document from inadvertant changes.

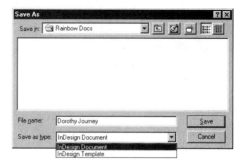

35 The **Save As** dialog box (Win).

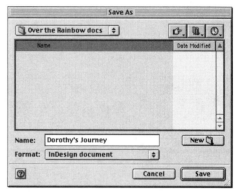

36 The **Save As** dialog box (Mac).

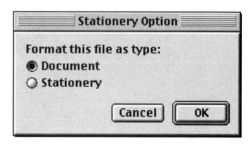

37 The **Stationery Option** dialog box (Mac).

It happens—someday, somehow your computer will crash or you will be forced to restart it without saving your work. Fortunately InDesign has an automatic recovery option that can save your work.

To recover a file:

1. Restart the computer after the crash or data loss.

2. Start InDesign.

3. If there is any automatic recovery information on the file, a dialog box appears asking if you want to update the file with the data.

   Click Yes to include any of the recovered information.

   Choose No to discard any of the recovered information.

4. Choose **File** >**Save As** to save the file with a new name and destination.

TIP The restored data is a temporary version of the file and must be saved in order to ensure the integrity of the data.

Saving Documents

TEXT 3

When I started in advertising around twenty-five years ago, setting type was an involved process. The copywriter would first type out the text on pieces of paper. An art director or typographer would then mark the page of copy up with a red pencil to indicate the typeface, point size, leading, and so on. The copy was sent to a typesetting house where a typesetter would retype the text into a special typesetting machine. The text would be printed onto special photographic paper and sent back the next morning. The copywriter would then have to proof the text to make sure that there were no errors.

That's why I am amazed every time I use a program such as InDesign to set text. I don't type onto a piece of paper; I type right onto my actual layout. I don't have to send the copy out overnight; it's right there on my computer screen. And I know that the only mistakes are the ones I make myself!

Creating Text Frames

InDesign contains all text within elements called *frames*.

To create a text frame with the Type tool:

1. Click the Type tool in the Toolbox ❶.

2. Move the cursor to the page area. The cursor changes to the Type tool cursor ❷.

3. Drag to create the text frame. A line appears indicating the size of the frame that will be created ❸.

TIP The text frame starts from the small horizontal line that intersects the text frame cursor.

TIP Hold the Shift key to constrain the text frame to a square.

4. Release the mouse button. The text frame appears with a blinking insertion point that indicates you can type in the frame.

To draw an elliptical frames:

1. Click the Ellipse tool in the Toolbox ❹.

2. Drag diagonally to create the ellipse.

TIP Hold the Shift key to constrain the ellipse into a circle.

3. Release the mouse button when the ellipse is the correct size.

To draw a rectangular frame:

1. Click the Rectangle tool in the Toolbox ❺.

2. Drag diagonally to create the rectangle.

TIP Hold the Shift key to constrain the rectangle into a square.

3. Release the mouse button when the rectangle is the correct size.

❶ Choose the **Type tool** in the Toolbox to work with text.

❷ The cursor set to create a text frame.

❸ Drag with the Type tool to create a text frame.

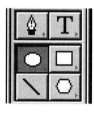

❹ The **Ellipse tool** in the Toolbox.

❺ The **Rectangle tool** in the Toolbox.

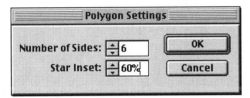

❻ The **Polygon tool** in the Toolbox.

❼ Use the **Polygon Settings** dialog box to change the shape and the number of sides of a polygon.

To draw a polygon frame:

1. Double-click the Polygon tool in the Toolbox ❻. This opens the Polygon Settings dialog box ❼.

2. Enter a number in the field for the number of sides.

3. To create a star, change the amount in the Star Inset field.

TIP A star inset of 0% creates a polygon. As you increase the number, points of the star become more obvious.

4. Drag across the page to create the polygon or star.

TIP Hold the Shift key to constrain the width and height of the object to the same amount.

5. Release the mouse button when the polygon or star is the correct size.

When you create frames with the Rectangle, Ellipse, and Polygon tools, you must convert them into text frames. Until you do, they are unassigned frames.

To convert unassigned frames:

1. Select the frame you want to convert.

2. Choose the Type tool and click inside the frame.

    or

    Choose **Object** > **Content** > **Text.**

    An insertion point appears indicating that you can begin typing.

TIP You can modify text frames in various ways; you can resize or reshape them just as other objects. *(For more information on changing the size and shape of text frames, see Chapter 4, "Working with Objects.")*

Creeating Text Frames

Typing Text

The two most important parts of working with text are typing the text and then selecting the text to make changes. If you are familiar with a word processing program such as Microsoft Word, or a page layout program such as QuarkXPress, you will find it very easy to type and select text in InDesign.

To type text:

1. Click with the Type tool in a frame.

2. Begin typing.

3. Press Return to begin a new paragraph.

   or

   Press Shift-Return to begin a new line without starting a new paragraph.

TIP InDesign automatically wraps text within the text frame.

TIP If the text frame is too small to display all the text, an overflow symbol ❽ appears. You can reshape the box (*see page 64*) or flow the text into a new frame (*see page 56*) to eliminate the overflow.

To add text into a passage you have already typed, you move the *insertion point* to where you want to insert the new material. The point blinks to help you find it ❾.

To move the insertion point:

1. Position the Type tool cursor where you want the insertion point.

2. Click to set the insertion point.

To move the point using the keyboard:

1. Use the arrow keys to move the insertion point left or right one character at a time or one line at a time.

2. Use the Command/Ctrl key with the arrow keys to move one word or one paragraph at a time.

> "See what you have done!" she screamed. "In a minute I shall melt away."
> "I'm very sorry, indeed," said Dorothy, who was truly frightened to see the Witch actually melting away like brown sugar before her very eyes.
> "Didn't you know water would be the ⊕

❽ The **overflow symbol** in a text frame

> "See what you have done!" she screamed. "In a minute I shall melt away."
> "I'm very sorry, indeed," said Dorothy,

❾ The **blinking insertion point** within text.

Keyboard, Mouse, or Menu?

One of the hot topics in designing software is the keyboard versus mouse debate. If you are a fast typist, you certainly work faster using keyboard shortcuts. There are times you should consider using a mouse.

I use the following guidelines. If my hands are already on the keyboard, I try to keep them there to select text or apply a formatting change.

But if my hands are on the mouse, I try to use it. So if I've just finished moving a text frame to a new position, I can easily highlight the text with the mouse.

Menu commands are another matter entirely. I try whenever possible to learn the keyboard shortcuts for menu commands. That way I don't have to move the mouse all the way up to the top of the page to choose a command.

Electronic Styling: Myths and Realities

As you set type using programs such as InDesign, people may tell you *never* to style fonts electronically. So if you use the Roman version of a font (such as Minion), you should never type the keyboard shortcut for italic. You should only choose the actual typeface (Minion Italic).

The rule emerged because some typefaces do not have an italic or bold version. The styling shows on the screen, but it doesn't print. Techno, or Zapf Dingbats are examples of fonts that you should not electronically style.

Fortunately, InDesign prevents you from making errors if you apply keyboard shortcuts for bold or italic. If you apply the shortcut for italic, InDesign applies the actual italic version. If there is no version, InDesign does not change the font.

Some people advise avoiding all caps, subscript, small caps, and other electronic styles. In most cases, there is nothing wrong with applying those styles, and InDesign allows you to apply those electronic styles no matter what font versions you have installed. In some cases you'll have better results with a small-caps version of a font than with the electronic style, but few fonts have small-caps versions, and few people recognize the difference. *(For an excellent discussion on how to use electronic small caps, see* The Non-Designer's Type Book *by Robin Wiliams.)*

Selecting Text

Although the simplest way to select text is to highlight the text, there are more sophisticated methods that allow you to select specific words, lines, or paragraphs. Although these may seem confusing at first, if you use the techniques often, they should become second nature.

To select text using the mouse:

◆ Drag across the text. The highlight indicates which text is being selected.

or

Double-click within a word to select it and the space following it.

or

Triple-click within a paragraph to select it.

If you are a fast typist you may find you work faster if you keep your fingers on the keyboard as you work with text. If so, try the keyboard shortcuts for selecting text.

To select text using keyboard shortcuts:

1. Hold down the Shift key and press an arrow key to move one character or one line at a time.

2. Hold down the Command/Ctrl+Shift keys and press an arrow key to move one word or one paragraph at a time.

3. Choose Command+A/Ctrl+A to select all the text within an entire text frame.

Moving and Deleting Text

You can copy text and put it elsewhere in your InDesign document. You can also copy and paste the text in one move by using the Duplicate command. Another advantage of copying with the Duplicate command is that it leaves the contents of the clipboard untouched. *(See the sidebar, "The Computer Clipboard," for an explanation of how the clipboard works.)*

To copy and paste text:

1. Select the text or text frame.

2. Choose **Edit > Copy**.

3. Position the insertion point where you want to put the copied text.

4. Choose **Edit > Paste**. The copied text is inserted into the new position ➓.

TIP You can select text and paste to replace the selected text with the copied text.

The Duplicate command copies and pastes in one step.

To duplicate text:

1. Select the text or text frame.

2. Choose **Edit > Duplicate**. The copied text is duplicated as follows:

   A text frame is created slightly offset from the original object.

   Text inside a frame is pasted immediately following the original text.

TIP The Duplicate command does not replace the contents of the clipboard.

To move text:

1. Select the text or text frame.

2. Choose **Edit > Cut**.

3. Move the insertion point to the place where you want the text inserted.

4. Choose **Edit > Paste**. The text is copied from the clipboard to the new location.

➓ The effects of the **copy and paste commands**.

The Computer Clipboard

The copy command places the copied objects into an area of the computer memory called the clipboard. The contents of the clipboard stay within the memory until a new copy or cut command is executed or the computer is turned off.

The clipboard can hold only one set of information at a time. So if you copy one sentence, you will lose it from the clipboard if you copy or cut something else later on.

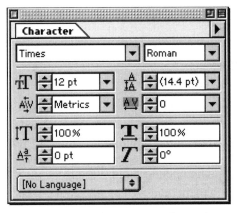

⑪ The **Character palette** lets you change the character attributes.

⑫ The Character palette in the **horizontal** and **vertical** orientations.

Using the Character Palette

Character formatting refers to attributes that can be applied to a single character in a paragraph. The Character palette controls character attributes.

To work with the Character palette:

1. If the Character palette is not visible, choose **Type** >**Character**. This opens the Character palette **⑪**.

   or

   Click the Character palette tab to move it to the front of a set of tabbed palettes.

2. To change the Character palette from horizontal to vertical orientation, choose Vertical Palette from the Character palette pop-up menu **⑫**.

3. To display all the character formatting controls choose Show Options from the Character palette pop-up menu.

Using the Character Palette

Setting the Typeface and Point Size

The look of type is called the typeface. This typeface is called Minion. The typeface of the subhead below is called Futura Condensed Bold.

To choose a font (typeface):

◆ Choose **Type** > **Font** and then choose the typeface from the font list

or

Choose a typeface from the font field pop-up list **13**.

13 The **Font field** in the Character palette.

14 The **Point size field** in the Character palette.

The size of type is measured using a system called *points.* There are 72 points per inch.The point size of this paragraph is 10.25.

TIP Traditional typesetting measured 72.27 points per inch. However, most electronic desktop publishing programs round that size off to 72 points per inch.

To change the point size:

◆ Choose **Type** > **Size** and then choose a point size from the list.

or

Use the point size field controls **14**.

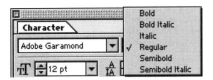

⓯ The **typeface styles** for Adobe Garamond as listed in the style field pop-up list.

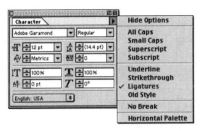

⓰ The **electronic style options** in the Character palette pop-up menu.

Dorothy and Toto
DOROTHY AND TOTO   All caps

L. Frank Baum
L. FRANK BAUM   Small caps

H2O
H₂O   Subscript

The Emerald City®
The Emerald City®   Superscript

The Cowardly Lion
The ~~Cowardly~~ Lion   Strike through

The Tin Woodman
The Tin Woodman   Underline

⓱ The effects of applying the electronic styles.

The first flush of spring
The first flush of spring

⓲ An example of ligatures.

Styling Text

There are two types of styles you can apply to text in InDesign: typestyle and electronic style. Typestyle refers to looks such as bold, italic, and condensed styles.

To set the typestyle:

◆ Choose a typeface style from the style field pop-up list **⓯**.

TIP The typestyle list changes depending on the typeface and the parts of the typeface you have installed. If you do not have the bold version of a font, it will not be listed.

InDesign also lets you apply electronic styling such as All Caps, Small Caps, Subscript, and Superscript.

To add electronic styles:

◆ Choose one of the styles listed in the Character palette pop-up menu **⓰**.

All Caps converts lowercase letters to all capital letters **⓱**.

TIP The All Caps style has no effect on text typed with the Caps Lock or Shift key held down.

Small Caps converts lowercase letters to reduced capital. *(See page 43 for a discussion about electronic styling.)*

Superscript reduces and raises the text above the baseline.

Subscript reduces and lowers the text below the baseline.

TIP The sizes of the Small Caps, Subscript, and Superscript are controlled in the type preferences *(see page 241)*.

Underline draws a line under the text.

Strikethrough draws a line through the text.

Ligatures automatically substitutes the combined letterforms for characters such as fi and fl **⓲**.

Setting Line and Character Spacing

Leading is the space between lines of type within a paragraph **19**. (It is pronounced *ledding*, which refers to the metal formerly used to set type.) In layout programs, leading is specified as a point size or auto leading. The leading of this paragraph is 10.75 points.

To set the leading:

1. Select the paragraph of text.

2. Use the leading field controls in the Character palette to enter an amount of leading.

   or

   Set the leading to auto to have the leading automatically change to an amount based on the point size.

TIP The amount of the auto leading is set in the Paragraph palette Justification submenu *(see page 184)*.

Kerning is the space between two letters. It is applied so letters fit snugly together **20**.

To set kerning:

1. To use the basic metric kerning pairs built into the typeface, choose Metrics from the kerning field list in the Character palette.

   or

   Choose Optics to adjust the kerning using the visual representation of the text.

TIP Use optical kerning when there are no built-in font metrics, for instance, when you combine two different typefaces **21**.

2. To apply absolute kerning, use the kerning controls or pop-up list to apply a numerical amount.

TIP Positive numbers increase the space between letters. Negative numbers decrease the space. Zero applies no kerning.

19 An example of different leading applied to text.

20 The effect of **kerning**.

21 How **optical kerning** changes the spacing between characters.

The Emerald City   No tracking

The Emerald City   +100 tracking

㉒ The effect of tracking.

Dial: (212)   No shift

Dial: (212)   +5 baseline shift

㉓ The effect of **baseline shift**.

㉔ The **baseline field** controls.

Tracking is similar to kerning; however, unlike kerning, tracking is applied to a range of letters **㉒**.

To set tracking:

1. Select the text you want to track.

2. Use the tracking field controls in the Character palette to set the amount of tracking.

TIP Positive numbers increase the space between letters. Negative numbers decrease the space. Zero applies no tracking.

Baseline shift moves text up or down from the baseline, or the imaginary line that the bottom of letters sit on. Baseline shift is often applied to shift bullets or parenthesis so they sit better next to text **㉓**.

To set the baseline shift:

1. Select the text that you want to reposition.

2. Use the baseline field controls **㉔** in the Character palette to move the text away from the baseline.

TIP Positive numbers move the text up. Negative numbers move the text down.

Applying Text Distortions

InDesign also lets you apply horizontal or vertical scaling to text. This distorts the text to increase its height or width . This changes the text from the original design of the characters. Typographic purists (such as this author) disdain distorting text.

To apply horizontal scaling:

1. Select the text that you want to distort.

2. Use the horizontal scale field controls  in the Character palette to change the width of the text.

To apply vertical scaling:

1. Select the text that you want to distort.

2. Use the vertical scale field controls  in the Character palette.

Skewing allows you to slant or tilt text 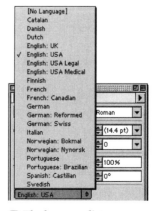. This is also called *false italic* because it resembles the slant of italic text.

To skew text:

1. Select the text that you want to skew.

2. Enter an angle in the skew field **29** in the Character palette of how much the text should be slanted.

TIP Positive numbers to 180 degrees tilt the text to the left. Negative numbers to 180 degrees tilt the text to the right.

Setting the Language

You can also set the language. This makes sure that foreign words are spell checked and hyphenated using the proper dictionary.

To set the language:

1. Select the text that you want to set the language for.

2. Choose the language from the pop-up list **30** in the Character palette.

Dorothy   75% vertical scale

Dorothy   No scaling

Dorothy   125% horizotnal scale

25 The effects of applying **horizontal or vertical scaling**.

26 The **horizontal scale field** controls.

27 The **vertical scale field** controls.

The
Cyclone !

28 The effect of **skewing text**.

29 The **skew field**.

30 The **language list**.

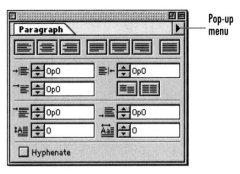

Pop-up menu

③ The **Paragraph palette**.

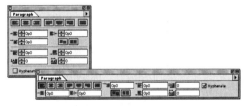

③ The Paragraph palette in the **horizontal** and **vertical** orientations.

Applying Paragraph Formatting

Paragraph formatting refers to the attributes that are applied to the paragraph as a whole. For instance, you cannot have half of the paragraph centered and the other half on the left size of the page. The alignment must be applied to the whole paragraph. InDesign paragraph formatting is applied using the Paragraph palette.

TIP The following techniques are useful when applying paragraph attributes:

- To apply attributes to a single paragraph, click to place the insertion point within the paragraph.

- To apply attributes to more than one paragraph, select a portion of the first and last paragraph and the paragraphs in between.

To work with the Paragraph palette:

1. If the Paragraph palette is not visible, choose **Type** > **Paragraph**. This opens the Paragraph palette **③**.

or

Click the Paragraph palette tab to move it to the front of a set of tabbed palettes.

2. To change the Paragraph palette from horizontal to vertical orientation, choose Vertical Palette from the Paragraph palette pop-up menu **③**.

3. To display all the paragraph formatting controls, choose Show Options from the Paragraph palette pop-up menu.

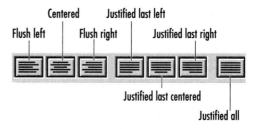

Setting Alignment and Indents

In addition to the common alignment controls found in page layout or word processing, InDesign offers some new controls for setting alignment.

To set paragraph alignment:

1. Select the paragraphs.

2. Click one of the seven Alignment buttons ❸❸ to set the alignment as follows:

   Flush Left ❸❹ sets the text to align at the left margin.

   Centered ❸❹ sets the text to align at the center of the paragraph.

   Flush Right ❸❹ sets the text to align at the right margin.

   Justified Last Left ❸❹ sets the text to align at both the left and right margins, but aligns the last line flush left.

   Justified Last Centered ❸❹ sets the text to align at both the left and right margins, but centers the last line.

   Justified Last Right ❸❹ sets the text to align at both the left and right margins, but aligns the last line flush right.

   Justified All ❸❹ sets all the text to align at both the left and right margins.

❸❸ The **Alignment buttons.**

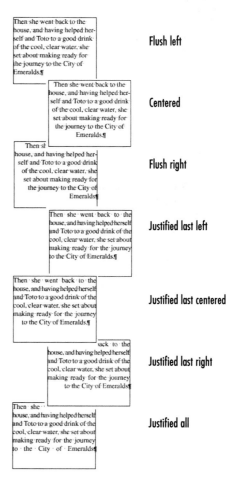

❸❹ Examples of the eight alignment settings.

Left   First line   Right

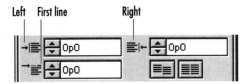

⬤ The margin indent controls.

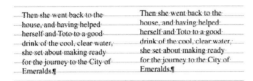

⬤ The effects of alignment to baseline grid.

On   Off

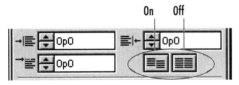

⬤ The buttons for baseline grid alignment.

The indent settings let you move text so that it is indented from the edges of the text frame.

To set the margin indents:

1. Select the paragraphs.

2. Set an amount with the margin indent controls ⬤ to move the text as follows:

    Left moves the left side of the paragraph away from the left side of the text frame.

    First Line moves the first line of the paragraph away from the rest of the paragraph.

    Right moves the right side of the paragraph away from the right side of the text frame.

The baseline grid is a set of electronic horizontal lines that cross the pages of your document. You can set text to always sit on one of the baselines. This ensures that two columns of text are always even ⬤.

To align to the baseline grid:

1. Select the paragraphs that you want to align to the baseline grid.

2. Click the align to baseline grid button so that it is in the On position ⬤. This forces the text to align to the closest line of the baseline grid. *(For more information on viewing grids, see Chapter 2, "Document Setup.")*

Alignment and Indents

Setting Paragraph Effects

The paragraph effects are available when Show Options is chosen in the Paragraph palette. They include space above and below, drop caps, and hyphenation.

To add space between paragraphs:

1. Select the paragraphs that you want to add space above or below.

2. Use the Space Before field controls ❸❽ to add space before the paragraphs.

3. Use the Space After field controls ❸❾ to add space after the paragraphs.

TIP Never insert paragraph returns to add space between paragraphs. That can cause problems later if text reflows!

A drop cap increases the first character or characters size and positions them so that the rest of the text wraps around them in the paragraph ❹⓿.

To create drop caps:

1. Select the paragraph you want to set with a drop cap.

2. Use the Drop Cap Number of Lines field ❹❶ to set the number of lines that the letter should be dropped down.

3. Use the Drop Cap Number of Characters field ❹❷ to set how many characters of the text should have the drop cap applied.

You can also control if the text within a paragraph should be hyphenated ❹❸.

To turn on hyphenation:

1. Select the paragraph you want to set the hyphenation for.

2. To turn on hyphenation, click hyphenate. *(For more information on working with hyphenation, see Chapter 10, "Advanced Text.")*

❸❽ The **Space Before** controls.

❸❾ The **Space After** controls.

D orothy·lived·in·the·midst·of the·great·Kansas·prairies,· with·Uncle·Henry,·who·was a·farmer,·and·Aunt·Em,·who·was·the farmer's·wife.·Their·house·was·small,·

❹⓿ An example of a **drop cap**.

❹❶ The **Drop Cap Number of Lines** field.

❹❷ The **Drop Cap Number of Characters** field.

Then she went back to the house, and having helped herself and Toto to a good drink of the cool, clear water, she set about making ready for the journey to the City of Emeralds.

❹❸ The effects of **hyphenating text**.

Decrease preview size

Increase preview size

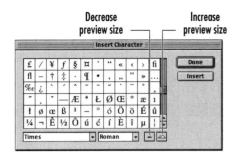

44 The **Insert Character** dialog box.

New paragraph

Tab   Space   New line

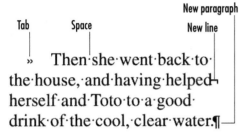

45 Hidden **characters** within text.

Using Text Utilities

The Insert Character utility lets you easily see all the characters in a typeface. This includes characters that are accessed using special modifiers.

To insert characters:

1. Place the insertion point where you would like the character to be inserted.

2. Choose **Type > Insert Character.** This opens the Insert Character dialog box **44**.

3. Choose the typeface and style of the character you want to insert.

4. Scroll through the Character Preview area to find the character you want to insert.

TIP Use the preview size controls to increase or decrease the size of the preview.

5. Chose the character you want to insert and then click the Insert button.

6. Insert any additional characters.

7. When you are finished, click the Done button to exit the dialog box.

TIP The Insert Character dialog box allows you to insert characters that are not usually available for certain operating systems. For instance, Macintosh users can insert fractions and Windows users can insert ligatures.

You can also display the hidden characters, (sometimes called *invisibles*) that let you know where spaces, tab characters, and paragraph returns are in the text.

To display hidden characters:

◆ Choose **Type > Show Hidden Characters.** This displays the characters in the same color as the highlight for the layer **45**. *(For more information on working with layers, see Chapter 8, "Long Documents.")*

Working with Text Flow

As mentioned earlier *(see page 42)*, if text overflows its text frame, you can link the text into another frame.

To link text between frames:

1. Click the overflow symbol in the text box. This changes the cursor to the load text cursor **46**.

2. Move the cursor over to the frame you want to flow the text into. The cursor changes to the link cursor **47**.

3. Click in the text frame. The link indicators **48** show that the text in the frame flows to or from another frame.

TIP You can use the same steps to link text frames that do not have any text in them. This makes it easy to flow text later into the layout.

To change the link between frames:

1. Click the link indicator in the frame where you want to break the link. The cursor turns into a link cursor.

2. Click in a new text frame to flow the text into a new frame.

    or

    Click inside the text frame to keep all the text within that frame. (The overflow symbol appears.)

InDesign also displays *text threads* which shown you the links between text frames

To show the links between frames:

1. Select the text frame that you want to see the links for.

2. Choose View>**Show Text Threads**. This displays lines that show which frames are linked together **49**.

"See what you have done!" she screamed. "In a minute I shall melt away."

"I'm very sorry, indeed," said Dorothy, who was truly frightened to see the Witch actually melting away like brown sugar before her very eyes.

"Didn't you know water would be the

46 The **load text cursor.**

"See what you have done!" she screamed. "In a minute I shall melt away."

"I'm very sorry, indeed," said Dorothy, who was truly frightened to see the Witch actually melting away like brown sugar before her very eyes.

"Didn't you know water would be the

47 The **link text cursor.**

---

end of me?" asked the Witch, in a wailing, despairing voice.

"Of course not," answered Dorothy. "How should I?"

"Well, in a few minutes I shall be all melted, and

you will have the castle to yourself. I

48 The **link indicators** in a text frame.

---

actually melting away like brown sugar before her very eyes.

"Didn't you know water would be the

end of me?" asked the Witch, in a wailing, despairing voice.

"Of course not," answered Dorothy.

49 The **text threads** show the links between frames

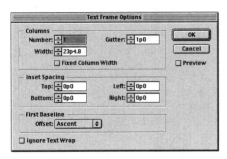

50 The **Text Frame Options** dialog box controls the flow of text within a frame.

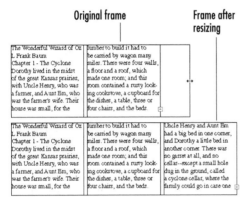

Original frame | Frame after resizing

51 The effect of setting the **Fixed Column Width** for a text frame.

Setting Text Frame Controls

Once you create a text frame, you can still control the flow of text within the frame. This is similar to creating a mini-layout within the text frame.

To create text frame columns:

1. Select the text frame.

2. Choose **Object >Text Frame Options**. This opens the Text Frame Options dialog box **50**.

3. Set the following options:

   The Number field sets the number of columns.

   The Width field sets the column width of the columns.

   The Gutter field controls the space between the columns.

4. Click the Preview checkbox to see the effects of the changes.

5. Click OK to apply the amounts.

InDesign also has a powerful feature that helps you maintain a fixed column width when working with a text frame. This is especially helpful for magazine and newspaper layouts where all text is in the same column width.

To use the fixed column width:

♦ Click Fixed Column Width in the Text Frame Options dialog box. As the frame is resized, the width automatically jumps to whatever size can contain an additional column **51**.

Setting Text Frame Controls

You can also control where the text is positioned within the frame. This is called the *inset spacing*.

To control the frame inset:

1. Select the text frame and open the Text Frame Options dialog box *(see page 57)*.

2. Enter the values in the Inset Spacing controls to control the amount of space between the top, bottom, left, and right edges of the frame **52**.

3. Click the Preview checkbox to see the effects of the changes.

4. Click OK to apply the changes to the column.

You can also control where the first baseline of the frame is positioned. (The *baseline* is the line on which the letters of the text rest.)

To control the first baseline:

1. Select the text frame and open the Text Frame Options dialog box *(see page 57)*.

2. Choose one of the three options in the Offset pop-up list.

   Ascent positions the first baseline so that the tops of the ascending characters (such as h, t, and d) are at the top edge of the text frame **53**.

   Cap Height positions the first baseline so that the tops of capital letters are at the top edge of the frame **53**.

   Leading positions the first baseline from the top edge at a distance equal to the leading assigned to the text **53**. *(See page 48 for more information on leading.)*

Dorothy lived in the midst of the great Kansas prairies, with Uncle Henry, who was a farmer, and Aunt Em, who was the farmer's wife. Their house was small, for the lumber to build it had to be carried by wagon many miles. There were four walls, a floor and a roof, which made one room; and this room contained a rusty looking cookstove, a cupboard for the dishes, a table,

52 The **Inset Frame controls** adds a space between the text frame and the text.

Uncle Henry — Ascent

Uncle Henry — Cap height

Uncle Henry — Leading

53 The **First Baseline** options control the position of the first line of the text.

WORKING WITH OBJECTS 4

Back in the old days of board mechanicals, advertising agencies and design studios had an production area called the *bullpen*. It was the people in the bullpen—called bullpen artists—who actually created the mechanical. Most of them were kids just out of design school; the bullpen was usually their first step up the ladder in advertising or design.

If we needed a simple shape—a line, a circle, a box—on the layout, it was no problem to ask the bullpen artist to draw the shape. Sometimes we could ask for more complicated artwork. At a certain point we had to stop asking the artists in the bullpen to do the work. We had to hire real artists to do the sophisticated illustrations.

The same is true with InDesign. While you can certainly use the program for drawing basic shapes, InDesign is not a full-fledged drawing program. For that you need a real illustration tool, such as Adobe Illustrator, CorelDraw or Macromedia FreeHand.

Creating Basic Shapes

Although InDesign is not a dedicated drawing program such as Adobe Illustrator, it does have a wide variety of tools to create graphic objects. The four tools for creating basic shapes are the Rectangle, Ellipse, Polygon, and Line tools.

TIP All four of the tools create objects that are unassigned. To convert the objects to text frames, see page 41. To convert the objects to graphic frames, see page 113.

InDesign also has a Pen tool that allows you to create more sophisticated shapes using Bézier controls. *(For more information on working with the Pen tool, see Chapter 5, "Pen and Béziers.")*

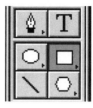

❶ The **Rectangle tool** in the Toolbox.

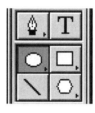

❷ The **Ellipse tool** in the Toolbox.

To create a rectangular frame:

1. Click the Rectangle tool in the Toolbox ❶.

2. Drag across the page to create the rectangle.

3. Release the mouse button when the rectangle is the correct size.

TIP Hold the Shift key to constrain the rectangle into a square.

To create an elliptical frame:

1. Click the Ellipse tool in the Toolbox ❷.

2. Drag across the page to create the ellipse.

3. Release the mouse button when the ellipse is the correct size.

TIP Hold the Shift key to constrain the ellipse into a circle.

Creating Basic Shapes

❸ The **Polygon tool** in the Toolbox.

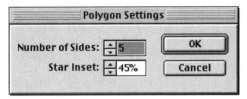

❹ The **Polygon Settings** dialog box.

❺ The **Line tool** in the Toolbox.

To create a polygon frame:

1. Double-click the Polygon tool in the Toolbox ❸. This opens the Polygon Settings dialog box ❹.

2. Enter a number in the field for the number of sides.

3. To create a star, change the amount in the Star Inset field.

TIP A star inset of 0% creates a polygon. As you increase the percentage, the points of the star become more obvious.

4. Drag across the page to create the polygon or star.

TIP Hold the Shift key to constrain the width and height of the object to the same amount.

5. Release the mouse button when the polygon or star is the correct size.

To create straight lines:

1. Click the Line tool in the Toolbox ❺.

2. Position the cursor where you want the line to start.

3. Drag to create a line.

4. Release the mouse where you want the line to end.

TIP Hold the Shift key to constrain the lines to 45-degree angles.

Creating Basic Shapes

Replicating Objects

The edit commands allow you to make copies of objects. These are the same commands found in almost all graphics programs.

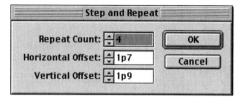

❻ The **Step and Repeat** dialog box.

Use Copy when you want to put the object on the clipboard so you can paste it somewhere else. *(See page 64 for how to copy an object as you move it.)*

To copy objects:

1. Select an object to copy.

2. Choose **Edit** > **Copy**.

To paste objects:

◆ Choose **Edit** > **Paste**. The contents of the clipboard appear in the center of the window area.

Use Duplicate when you want to make a copy without changing the clipboard.

To duplicate objects:

1. Choose the object to duplicate.

2. Choose **Edit** > **Duplicate**. The selected object appears on the page.

You can also make many duplicates at once.

To duplicate multiple objects:

1. Choose an object.

2. Choose **Edit** > **Step and Repeat**. The Step and Repeat dialog box appears **❻**.

3. In the Repeat Count field, enter the number of duplicates to create.

4. In the Horizontal Offset field, enter a distance for the horizontal space between duplicates.

5. In the Vertical Offset field, enter a distance for the vertical space between duplicates.

6. Click OK. The selected object is duplicated in the desired positions.

Replicating Objects

❼ The **Selection tool** in the Toolbox.

Marquee   Objects to be selected

❽ Drag to create a **marquee** to select objects.

Selecting Objects

Once you have created objects, you can use different techniques to select those objects.

To select by clicking:

1. Choose the Selection tool in the Toolbox **❼**.

2. Click the object you want to select.

3. Hold the Shift key to select any additional objects.

TIP Hold the Shift key and click on a selected object to deselect that object.

TIP To select objects behind others, hold the Command/Ctrl key as you click the mouse button.

You can also select objects by dragging a dotted line, or *selection marquee,* around the object.

To select by dragging a marquee:

1. Choose the Selection tool.

2. Drag along a diagonal angle to create a marquee around the objects you want to select **❽**.

TIP You do not need to marquee the entire object to select it. Objects are selected if any portion is within the marquee.

TIP Hold the Shift key and drag around another area to add to a selection.

You can also use a menu command to select all the objects on a page.

To select all the objects on a page:

♦ Choose Edit > Select All.

TIP This command works only if you do not have an insertion point blinking inside a text frame. *(For more information on working with text, see Chapter 3, "Text.")*

Selecting Objects

Moving and Resizing Objects

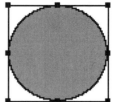

❾ The **bounding box** for a selected object.

The simplest way to position an object on a page is to drag it to a new position.

To move an object by dragging:

1. Choose the Selection tool in the Toolbox.

2. Click the object you want to move. A bounding box with eight handles appears around the object **❾**. This indicates the object is selected.

3. Position the Selection tool on the edges of the bounding box (but not the handles of the bounding box).

TIP If an object has a fill color, gradient, or image inside it, you can drag the Selection tool directly inside the object. Otherwise, you must drag the stroke or bounding box.

4. Drag to move the object.

TIP Hold the Option/Alt key down to both move and create a copy of the object.

You can also use the bounding box handles to change the dimensions of the object visually.

To resize an object by dragging:

1. Choose the Selection tool.

2. Drag one of the handles of the bounding box. Decide which handle to drag based on the following options:

   • Drag the corner handles to change both the width and height.

   • Drag the top or bottom handles to change the height only.

   • Drag the left or right handles to change the width only.

TIP Hold down the Shift key as you drag a corner to keep the original proportions of the width and height.

Warning: Watch Out When You Scale or Shear!

Scaling or shearing can change the shape of objects as well as their contents. For instance, if you scale up a text frame 150%, the point size also increases 150%. Unfortunately, the changes do not show in the Character palette. So text that is listed as 12 point actually prints as 18 point.

Similar changes happen to strokes applied to objects. The size of the stroke weight can change but the change is not shown in the Stroke palette.

Unless you are very sure of what you are doing, it is a good idea to avoid scaling or shearing text or strokes. However, there is no problem resizing an object using the bounding box handles.

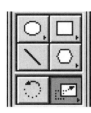

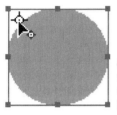

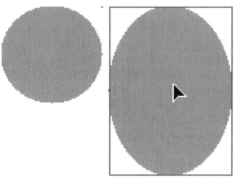

🔟 The **Scale tool** in the Toolbox.

⓫ The indicator that the **transformation point** can be moved to a new position.

⓬ The **curved arrowhead** appears while scaling an object.

Using the Transform Tools

InDesign also has several tools that let you transform shapes visually: the Scale tool, the Rotation tool, and the Shear tool. All transformations take place in relation to a *transformation point.* Each object has a default transformation point, but you can change it if necessary.

The Scale tool increases or decreases the size of objects. *(See the sidebar on the preceding page for a caution about working with the Scale tool.)*

TIP The InDesign Scale tool changes the point size of text, the size of placed images, and the width of strokes of objects that are scaled.

To use the Scale tool:

1. Select the object or objects you want to scale.

2. Click the Scale tool in the Toolbox **🔟**.

3. If necessary, change the default transformation point by dragging it to a new position **⓫**.

4. Move the cursor away from the transformation point, and drag to scale the object **⓬**.

TIP Hold down the Shift key to constrain the tool to horizontal, vertical, or proportional scaling.

TIP To see a preview of the image as you scale, press and hold the mouse button for a moment before you start to drag.

TIP Hold down the Option/Alt key to copy the object as you scale it.

The Rotation tool changes the orientation of objects.

To use the Rotation tool:

1. Select an object or objects.

2. Click the Rotation tool in the Toolbox 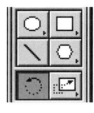.

⓲ The **Rotation tool** in the Toolbox.

3. If necessary, change the default transformation point by dragging it to a new position. The cursor changes to indicate the transformation point can be moved.

4. Move the cursor away from the transformation point, and drag to rotate the object ⓮.

TIP Hold down the Shift key to constrain the rotation to 45-degree increments.

TIP Hold down the Option/Alt key to copy the object as you rotate it.

⓮ Rotating an object around the transformation point.

The Shear tool distorts the shape of objects. *(See the sidebar on page 64 for a caution about working with the Shear tool.)*

To use the Shear tool:

1. Select an object or objects.

2. Click the Shear tool in the Toolbox ⓯.

3. If necessary, change the transformation point by dragging it to a new position. The cursor changes to indicate the transformation point can be moved.

4. Move the cursor away from the transformation point, and drag to shear the object ⓰.

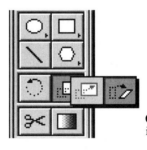
⓯ The **Shear tool** in the Toolbox.

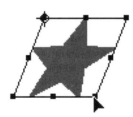
⓰ Shearing an object around the transformation point.

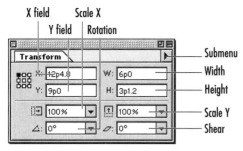

X field   Scale X
   Y field   Rotation

— Submenu
— Width
— Height
— Scale Y
— Shear

⑰ The Transform palette.

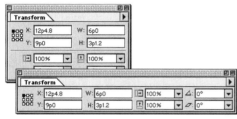

⑱ The **vertical and horizontal displays** of the Transform palette.

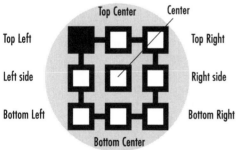

Top Center   Center

Top Left   Top Right

Left side   Right side

Bottom Left   Bottom Right

Bottom Center

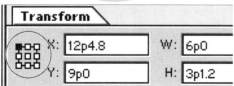

⑲ The **Reference point** controls where in the object the transformation occurs.

Using the Transform Palette

The Transform palette allows you to move, scale, rotate, and shear objects precisely, using numerical values.

To open the Transform palette:

◆ Choose **Window**>**Transform** to open the palette **⑰**.

or

If the Transform palette is behind other palettes, click the Transform palette tab.

To set the palette orientation:

◆ Choose Vertical palette or Horizontal palette from the submenu **⑱**.

To set the transform point:

1. Select the object you want to move.

2. Click the reference point control to choose what point of the object the move coordinates should control **⑲**.

To move an object with the Transform palette:

1. Select the object you want to move.

2. To move the object horizontally, enter an amount in the X field.

TIP As you increase the numbers, the object moves to the right.

3. To move the object vertically, enter an amount in the Y field.

TIP As you increase the numbers, the object moves down.

4. Press Enter or Return to apply the changes.

You can also resize objects using the Transform palette.

To resize with the Transform palette:

1. Select an object or objects.

2. If necessary, change the reference point as explained on the preceding page.

3. To change the width of the object, enter an amount in the **W** field.

4. To change the height of the object, enter an amount in the **H** field.

5. Press Enter or Return.

You can also scale objects using the Transform palette. *(See the warning about scaling objects in the sidebar on page 64.)*

To scale with the Transform palette:

1. Select an object or objects.

2. If necessary, change the reference point as explained on the preceding page.

3. To change the horizontal size, enter an amount in the **scale X** field.

4. To change the height of the object, enter an amount in the **scale Y** field.

TIP The **scale X** and **Y** fields also have pop-up lists to choose for the scaling.

5. Press Enter or Return ㉠.

㉠ The effect of scaling an object. Notice that the size of the text inside the object changes.

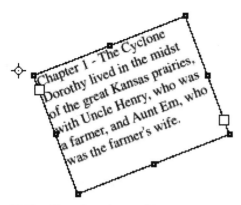

㉑ The effect of rotating an object.

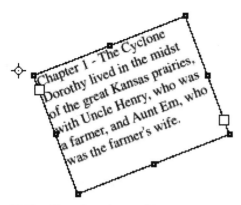

㉒ The effect of shearing an object.

You can also rotate objects using the Transform palette.

To rotate with the Transform palette:

1. Select the object or objects.

2. If necessary, change the reference point, as explained on page 67.

3. Enter the amount of rotation in the rotation field.

TIP The rotation field also has a pop-up list to choose for the rotation.

4. Press Enter or Return **㉑**.

You can also shear objects using the Transform palette. *(See the warning about shearing objects in the sidebar on page 64.)*

To shear with the Transform palette:

1. Select the object or objects you want to shear.

2. If necessary, change the reference point, as explained on page 67.

3. Enter the amount of distortion in the shear field.

TIP The shear field also has a pop-up list of amounts to choose for the distortion.

4. Press Enter or Return to apply the changes **㉒**.

Using the Transform Submenu

The Transform palette also gives you submenu commands that make it easy to perform commonly used transformations, such as rotating and flipping objects.

To rotate with the Transform submenu:

1. Select an object or objects.

2. Choose one of the rotation settings in the Transform submenu ㉓:

   • Rotate 180°.

   • Rotate 90° CW (clockwise).

   • Rotate 90° CCW (counter-clockwise).

To flip objects using the Transform submenu:

1. Select an object or objects.

2. Choose one of the flip settings in the Transform submenu ㉔:

   • Flip Horizontal.

   • Flip Vertical.

   • Flip Both.

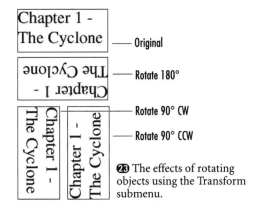

— Original
— Rotate 180°
— Rotate 90° CW
— Rotate 90° CCW

㉓ The effects of rotating objects using the Transform submenu.

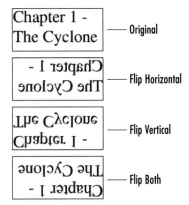

— Original
— Flip Horizontal
— Flip Vertical
— Flip Both

㉔ The effects of flipping objects using the Transform submenu.

㉕ When two objects overlap, it is obvious which object is is front of the other.

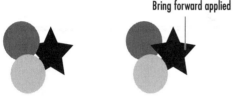

Bring forward applied

㉖ The effects of the **Bring Forward** command.

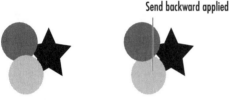

Send backward applied

㉗ The effects of the **Send Backward** command.

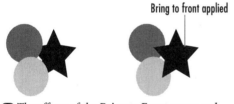

Bring to front applied

㉘ The effects of the **Bring to Front** command.

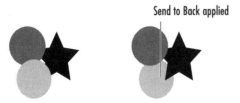

Send to Back applied

㉙ The effects of the **Send to Back** command.

Using the Arrange Commands

Objects in InDesign are layered on top of one other in the same order they were created. (This is sometimes called the *stacking order.*) The first object created is layered behind the second, and so on. Though you may not see the layering when objects are side by side, it is apparent when they overlap **㉕**.

TIP The layering of objects is not the same as the layers of a document. *(For more information on working with layers, see Chapter 8, "Long Documents.")*

The Arrange commands allow you to move objects through the stacking order.

To move up or down one level in a layer:

1. Select the object you want to move.

2. Choose **Object** > **Arrange** > **Bring Forward** to move the object in front of the next object in the stacking order **㉖**.

   or

   Choose **Object** > **Arrange** > **Send Backward** to move the object behind the next object in the stacking order **㉗**.

To move up or down the entire layer:

1. Select an object you want to move.

2. Choose **Object** > **Arrange** > **Bring to Front** to move the object in front of all the others in its layer **㉘**.

   or

   Choose **Object** > **Arrange** > **Send to Back** to move the object behind all the others in its layer **㉙**.

Aligning Objects

The Align palette provides commands that align objects or distribute them evenly along a horizontal or vertical axis.

To work with the Align palette:

1. Choose **Window > Align**. This opens the Align palette ③⓪.

   or

   If the Align palette is behind other palettes, click the Align palette tab.

2. Choose Show Options from the Align palette submenu to see all the commands in the palette.

To align objects:

1. Select two or more objects.

2. Click an alignment icon as follows:

   • Click a vertical alignment icon to move the objects into top, centered, or bottom alignment ③①.

   • Click a horizontal alignment icon to move the objects into left, centered, or right alignment ③②.

TIP The align commands move objects based on the best representative of the controls. For instance, the Align Left command uses the left-most object; Align Top uses the top-most object, and so on.

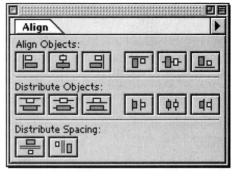

③⓪ The **Align** palette.

③① The effects of the **vertical align commands**.

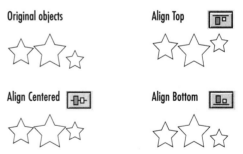

③② The effects of the **horizontal align commands**.

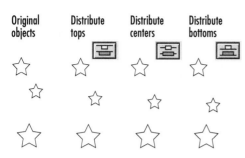

Original objects | **Distribute tops** | **Distribute centers** | **Distribute bottoms**

❸❸ The effects of the **vertical distribute commands.** Notice that the middle object changes position to create an even distribution of space.

Original objects | **Distribute left edges**

Distribute centers | **Distribute right edges**

❸❹ The effects of the **horizontal distribute commands.** Notice that the middle object changes position to create an even distribution of space.

Original objects | **Distribute vertical space**

❸❺ The effect of the **vertical distribute space** command.

Original objects | **Distribute horizontal space**

❸❻ The effects of the **horizontal distribute space** commands.

You can also move objects so the spaces between certain points of the objects are equal. This is call distributing objects.

To distribute objects:

1. Select three or more objects.

2. Click a distribute icon as follows:

   Click a vertical distribute icon to move the objects so that their tops, centers, or bottoms are equally distributed ❸❸.

   Click a horizontal distribute icon to move the objects so that their left edges, centers, or right edges are equally distributed ❸❹.

You can also distribute objects based on their absolute size. This ensures that the space between the objects is equal.

To distribute the space between objects:

1. Select three or more objects.

2. Click a distribute space icon as follows:

   Click the vertical space icon to move objects so the vertical spaces are equal ❸❺.

   Click the horizontal space icon to move objects so the horizontal spaces are equal ❸❻.

Alinging Objects

Grouping Objects

You can group objects so you can easily select and modify them as a unit.

To group objects:

1. Select the objects you want to group.

2. Choose **Object** > **Group**. A bounding box encloses all the objects 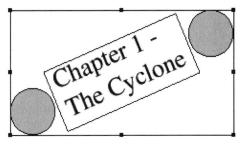.

TIP The Selection tool selects all the objects in a group as a single unit.

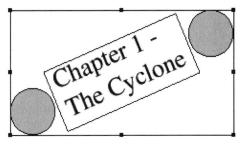
37 The **bounding box** around grouped objects.

You can also create groups within groups. This is called *nesting*.

To nest groups:

1. Select the grouped objects.

2. Hold the Shift key and select another object or group.

3. Choose **Object** > **Group**.

38 The **Direct Selection tool** in the Toolbox.

Once you have grouped objects, you can select individual objects within the group.

To select objects within groups:

1. Choose the Direction Selection tool **38**.

2. Click to select one object within the group.

3. Hold down the Option/Alt key and click the same object again **39**. This selects the entire group.

4. If the group is nested within other groups, click again on the same object to select the next level of the nest.

TIP Too many levels of nested groups may cause printing problems.

First click   Second click

39 Selecting **nested groups**.

To ungroup objects:

1. Select the group.

2. Choose **Object** > **Ungroup**.

3. If you have nested groups, continue to ungroup the objects as necessary.

Grouping Objects

40 The **padlock icon** indicates the object is locked.

Locking Objects

You can also lock objects so they cannot be moved or modified. This prevents people from inadvertently moving objects.

TIP Locking objects is not the same as locking the layers of a document. *(For more information on working with layers, see Chapter 8, "Long Documents.")*

To lock the position of an object:

1. Select the objects you want to lock.

2. Choose **Object >Lock Position.** A small padlock appears if you try to move or modify the object **40**.

TIP Locked objects can be selected, copied, pasted, and their colors and contents can be modified.

To unlock objects:

1. Select the objects you want to unlock.

2. Choose **Object >Unlock Position.**

Creating Fill Effects

Fills are the effects applied inside frames.

To apply a fill to an object:

1. Select an object.

2. Click the Fill icon in the Toolbox or Color palette **41**.

3. To apply a color fill, click the color in the Color or Swatches palette. *(For more information on the Color or Swatches palettes, see Chapter 6, "Working in Color.")*

You can also apply a fill of None to an object. This makes the background of the object transparent **42**.

To apply a fill of None:

1. Select the object.

2. Click the None icon in the Toolbox or Color palette **43**.

A compound path is a special effect applied to two paths that allows you set the inside path to appear transparent while the outside path has a solid background **44**.

To create a compound path:

1. Select two paths.

2. Choose **Object** > **Compound Paths** > **Make**.

TIP If the second object is not completely contained inside the first, the hole will appear where the objects overlap.

TIP Compound paths must contain the same fill and stroke effects.

You can release a compound path to restore the inside path to a solid color.

To release a compound path:

1. Select compound path.

2. Choose **Object** > **Compound Paths** > **Release**.

41 The **Fill icon** in the Toolbox and Color palette.

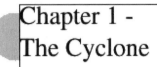

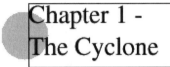

42 The difference between a text frame with a fill of None and a white fill.

43 The **None icon** in the Toolbox and Color palette.

44 The **compound path command** allows the text to be seen through the hole in the ellipse.

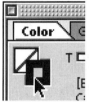

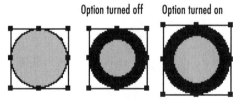 The **Stroke icon** in the Toolbox and Color palette.

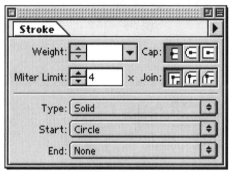

46 The Stroke palette.

Option turned off   Option turned on

47 When the **Weight Changes Bounding Box command** is chosen, increasing the stroke weight increases the size of the object.

Applying Stroke Effects

Strokes are the effects applied to the outside of objects and along lines.

To apply a stroke:

1. Select the object.

2. Click the Stroke icon in the Toolbox or Color palette **45**.

3. To apply a color stroke, click the color in the Color or Swatches palette. *(For more information on the Color or Swatches palettes, see Chapter 6, "Working in Color.")*

You can also apply special effects using the Stroke palette.

To work with the Stroke palette:

1. If the Stroke palette is not visible, choose **Window > Stroke** to view the Stroke palette **46**.

   or

   If the Stroke palette is behind other palettes, click the Stroke palette tab.

2. To display all the stroke controls, choose Show Options from the Stroke palette pop-up menu.

The weight of the stroke is the thickness of the stroke.

To set the stroke weight (thickness):

1. Select the object.

2. Use the weight field controls the set the thickness of the stroke.

3. To have the stroke weight increase the size of the bounding box, choose Weight Changes Bounding Box from the Stroke palette submenu **47**.

Applying Stroke Effects

The end caps and joins of a stroke control how the ends and points of the object are treated.

To set the caps and joins:

1. Select an object.

2. In the Stroke palette, use the Cap icons ⓭ to change the way the ends of open paths are treated:

   • Choose Butt to end the stroke in a square shape ⓮.

   • Choose Round to end the stroke in a semi-circle shape ⓮.

   • Choose Projecting to end the stroke in a square shape, the same size as the weight of the stroke ⓮.

TIP The Cap settings have no effect on closed paths such as rectangles, ellipses, and polygons.

3. Use the Join icons ⓯ to change the way two segments of a path meet at corners:

   • Choose Miter to join the segments at an angle ⓰.

   • Choose Round to join the segments with a curve.

   • Choose Bevel to join the segments with a line between the segments.

TIP The join commands affect only corner points. *(For more information on the different types of points, see Chapter 5, "Pen and Béziers.")*

Butt Round Projecting

⓭ The Cap icons.

⓮ The effects of the three cap settings.

Miter Round Bevel

⓯ The Join icons.

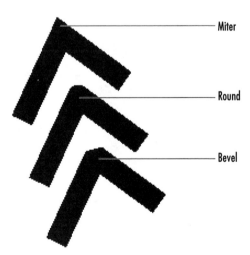

⓰ The effects of the three cap settings.

Miter limit 9

Miter limit 4

52 The effect of changing the miter limit.

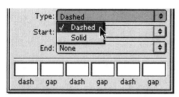

53 The **dashed settings** in the Stroke palette.

54 Various effects can be created using the dash and gap fields.

55 The effect of using the round cap on the dash settings.

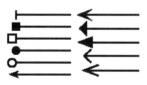

56 The built-in arrowheads and end shapes.

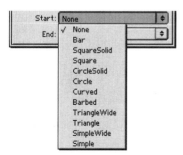

57 The **Arrow shapes** pop-up list.

If you set the join to the miter setting, you can control the limit of the angle created between two segments.

To set the miter limit:

1. Select an object with a mitered join.

2. In the Stroke palette, increase the amount in the Miter limit field to control the size of the angle between the segments.

TIP If the size of the angle exceeds the miter limit, a bevel is substituted **52**.

You can set strokes to be solid or dashed. If a stroke is set to dashed, you can set the size of the dashes and the gaps between them.

To create dashed strokes:

1. Select an object or objects.

2. Choose Dashed from the Type pop-up menu. The dashed settings appear at the bottom of the Stroke palette **53**.

3. Enter an amount in the first dash field for the length of the dash.

4. Enter an amount in the first gap field for the size of the space between the dashes.

5. To create different series of dashes and gaps, enter other values in the rest of the dash and gaps fields **54**.

TIP Apply round caps to create round ends to the dashes **55**.

You can also add arrowheads and other end shapes to the end of lines and open paths **56**.

To add arrowheads and end shapes:

1. Select an object.

2. Add a graphic to the beginning of the object, by choosing a shape from the Start pop-up list **57**.

3. Add a graphic to the end of the object, by choosing a shape from the End pop-up list.

Applying Stroke Effects

Adding Corner Effects

InDesign can modify the shape of objects by adding special corner effects. You can apply these effects to any object that has corner points, rather than smooth points. *(For more information on the difference between corner and smooth points, see Chapter 5, "Pen and Béziers.")*

To apply corner effects:

1. Select an object with corner points.

2. Choose **Object** > **Corner Effects**. The Corner Effects dialog box appears **58**.

3. Choose one of the effects from the Effect pop-up list **59**.

4. Set the size of the effect.

TIP Check Preview so you can see how the settings look.

5. Click OK to apply the settings.

TIP You can change corner effects later by selecting the object and reopening the dialog box. However, the actual points of the effect cannot be manipulated.

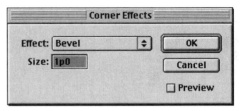

58 The **Corner Effects** dialog box.

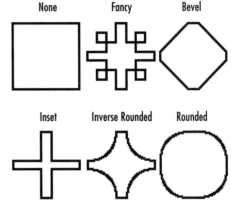

59 The different corner effects.

Adding Corner Effects

Setting Object Defaults

You can make any of the object settings the default for any new objects you create. You can set the object defaults for the current document or globally for all new documents.

To set current document defaults:

1. With a document open, deselect any objects.

2. Make whatever changes you want in the Stroke palette or other palettes. This sets the defaults for the open document.

To set global defaults:

◆ With no document open, make whatever changes you want in the Stroke or other palettes. This sets the global defaults for all new documents.

PEN AND BEZIERS 5

I remember the first time I tried to use the Pen tool in a computer graphics program. I clicked the tool and dragged across the screen in the way I thought would create a simple curve. Instead, I got a wild series of lines that shot out in different directions. When I tried to change the shape of the curves, things got even worse. I was so startled I immediately closed up the program and didn't use the Pen tool for a long, long time.

When I finally got up enough nerve to try the tool again, it took a lot of trial and error but eventually I was able to understand the Pen and Bézier controls. Once I got it, I realized the principles are simple. I just wish someone had written out easy to understand, step-by-step instructions. So think of this chapter as the instructions on the Pen tool that I wish I had back then.

Pen Points

One of the most important tools in any graphics program is the Pen tool. Fortunately InDesign has a similar Pen tool. This lets you create much more sophisticated shapes than can be created with the basic shape tools. *(For more information on working with the basic shapes, see Chapter 4, "Working with Objects.")* If you are familiar with the Pen tool in Adobe Illustrator or Macromedia FreeHand, you will find it very easy to master the Pen in InDesign.

If you've never used a Pen tool in any graphics program, you will understand more if you first become familiar with the elements of paths.

Elements of Paths

- Anchor points define a path at points where the path changes 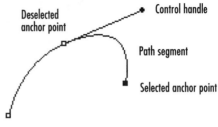.

- Segments are the paths that connect anchor points ❶.

- Control handles extend out from anchor points; their length and direction control the shape of curves of the segments ❶.

❶ The elements of a path.

The Father of Bézier Curves

Some people call the curves created by the Pen tool *Bézier curves*. This is in honor of Pierre Bézier (Bay-zee-ay), the French mathematician.

Monsieur Bézier created the system of mathematics that is used to define the relationship of the control handles to the shape of the curve.

Adobe Systems, Inc., adopted this mathematical system when it created the PostScript language which is used as the basis of graphics programs. InDesign, along with many other programs, uses Bézier curves as the mathematics behind each curve.

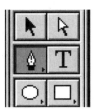

② Click the **Pen tool** in the Toolbox to create lines.

③ The **start icon** for the Pen tool.

④ Click with the Pen tool to create a **corner point,** shown as a small square.

⑤ Straight lines extend between the plain corner points.

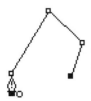

⑥ The small circle next to the Pen cursor indicates that you will close the path.

Drawing Lines

Different types of anchor points create different line shapes. Straight lines are formed by creating *plain corner points.*

To create straight lines:

1. Click the Pen tool in the Toolbox **②**.

2. Position the cursor where the path should start. A small *X* appears next to the Pen which indicates that you are starting the path **③**.

3. Click. A plain corner point appears as a colored square **④**.

4. Position the cursor for the next point and click. This creates another plain corner point with a straight line that connects the first point to the second.

TIP Hold the Shift key to constrain the straight lines to 45-degree angles.

5. Continue clicking until you have created all the straight-line sides of the object **⑤**.

TIP To start a new path, hold the Command/Ctrl key and click with the Selection tool. This deselects the path and allows you to start a new one.

To close a path with a straight line:

1. Move the Pen over the first point. A small circle appears next to the Pen **⑥**. This indicates that you can close the path.

2. Click. This closes the path with a plain corner point and allows you to start a new path.

Drawing Lines

Drawing Curves

Smooth curve points create curves like the track a roller coaster follows. There are no abrupt changes from one curve to another.

To create smooth curves:

1. With the Pen tool active, position the cursor where you want to start the curve and drag. Handles extend out from the smooth curve point.

2. Release the mouse button. The length and direction of the handle controls the height and direction of the curve.

   TIP You will not see a curve until you create the next point of the path.

3. Move the cursor to where you want the next part of the curve. Drag to create the curved segment between the two smooth curve points ❼.

4. Continue to create curved segments by repeating steps 2 and 3 ❽.

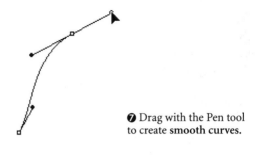

❼ Drag with the Pen tool to create **smooth curves.**

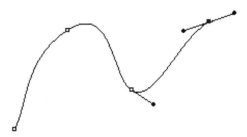

❽ A path with a series of curved segments.

To close a path with a smooth curve:

1. Move the Pen over the first point. A small circle appears indicating that you can close the path.

2. Drag backwards to close the path and create the control handle from the anchor point ❾.

A corner curve creates curves with an abrupt change in direction. The path of a bouncing ball illustrates a corner curve.

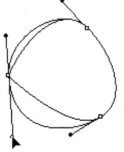

❾ Dragging backwards **closes a path with a smooth curve.**

To create a corner curve:

1. With the Pen tool active, drag to create an anchor point with control handles.

2. Without releasing the mouse button, hold the Option/Alt key and then drag to pivot the second handle ❿. This creates the corner curve point.

3. Release the mouse button when the second handle is the correct length and direction.

❿ Hold the Option/Alt key to pivot the handles, which creates a **corner curve.**

⓫ Move the cursor back over a point and click to **retract a handle** along a curve.

⓬ Drag with the Pen tool over an existing anchor point to **extend a handle** out from the point.

Changing Curves and Corner Points

If you retract the handle that extends out from a curve point, the next segment becomes a straight line.

To retract a handle:

1. Drag to create a smooth curve point.

2. Move the Pen cursor back over the anchor point. A small angle symbol appears next to the cursor.

3. Click. The handle retracts back into the anchor point ⓫. The point is now a corner point with only one handle.

4. Continue the path with either a straight line or a curved line.

TIP Click to make the next path segment straight. Drag to make the next path segment curved.

If you create a corner point with no control handles, you can extend a single handle out from that anchor point.

To extend a handle from a point:

1. Click to create a corner point with no handles.

2. Move the Pen cursor back over the anchor point you just created. A small angle symbol appears next to the cursor.

3. Drag to pull a single handle out from the anchor point ⓬.

4. Continue the path with a curved line.

General Pen Rules

As you work with the Pen tool, there are some general rules you should follow:

Use the smallest number of points to define a path. Too many points add to the size of the file and make it difficult to edit the path later.

Try to limit the length of the control handles to one-third the length of the curve. This is sometimes called the *One-Third Rule*. The One-Third Rule makes it easier to edit and control the shape of curves.

Modifying Paths

Once you create a path, you can still change its shape and the position of the points. You can also split a path into two separate segments or joint two segments together.

When you move points, you use the Direct Selection tool.

To move individual points:

1. Click the Direct Selection tool in the Toolbox **13**.

2. Position the tool over the point you want to move.

3. Drag the point to the new position.

The Direct Selection tool also lets you change the length and direction of the control handles.

To move control handles:

1. Click the Direct Selection tool.

2. Click a point on the path. This displays the control handles for that point.

3. Position the Direct Selection tool over the end point of the handle.

4. Drag the handle to the new position **14**.

13 The **Direct Selection tool** in the Toolbox; use it to move points.

14 The Direct Selection tool **changes the length and position of a control handle.**

15 The **Scissors tool** in the Toolbox allows you to snip paths in two.

16 The Scissors tool splits a path into two points, one on top of the other.

17 The results of applying the **Reverse Path** command to a path with an arrowhead.

To split paths:

1. Select the path.

2. Click the Scissors tool in the Toolbox **15**.

3. Position the cursor where you want to split the path.

4. Click to split the path at that point.

TIP The Scissors tool splits the path by creating two points, one on top of the other. Use the Direct Selection tool to move one point away from the other **16**.

TIP Paths that contain text cannot be split into two distinct segments.

The direction of a path comes from the order in which you draw the path. You can change the direction of the path.

To change the path direction:

1. Use the Direct Selection tool to select the path.

2. Choose **Object > Reverse Path.** This switches the start and end points of the path **17**.

Modifying Points

So what happens if you create the wrong point with the Pen tool? Are you stuck? Does it mean you have to redraw the entire path? Thankfully, no—there are many ways to change path points. So not only can you fix the mistakes you may have made with the Pen tool, but you can also modify basic shapes created with the other tools *(For more information on working with the basic shapes, see Chapter 4, "Working with Objects.")*

You may find that you want to add a point to a path. This helps you turn one shape into another.

To add points to a path:

1. Select the path.

2. Choose the Add Anchor Point tool in the Toolbox **⑱**.

3. Click the path where you want to add the point.

TIP The Pen tool automatically changes to the Add Anchor Point tool when positioned over a path segment.

You can also delete points from a path. This makes it easier to manipulate the path into different shapes.

To delete points from a path:

1. Select the path.

2. Choose the Delete Anchor Point tool in the Toolbox **⑲**.

3. Click to delete the point of the path.

TIP The Pen tool changes to the Delete Anchor Point tool when positioned over a point of a path segment.

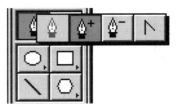

⑱ The **Add Anchor Point tool** in the Toolbox.

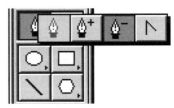

⑲ The **Delete Anchor Point tool** in the Toolbox.

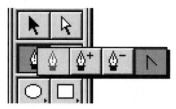

⑳ The **Convert Direction Point tool** in the Toolbox.

You can also change the control handles around an anchor point. This changes the shape of the segments controlled by that anchor point.

To modify an anchor point:

1. Select the path.

2. Choose the Convert Direction Point tool in the Toolbox **⑳**.

3. Use the tool as follows to change the anchor points:

   • Press and drag a corner point to create a smooth curve point with two handles **㉑**.

   • Click a smooth curve point to create a corner point with no handles **㉒**.

   • Drag one of the handles of a smooth curve point to create a corner curve point **㉓**.

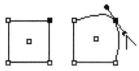

㉑ Drag with the Convert Direction Point tool to change a corner point into a smooth curve point.

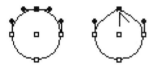

㉒ Click with the Convert Direction Point tool to change a smooth curve point into a corner point.

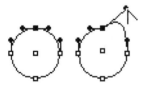

㉓ Drag a handle with the Convert Direction Point tool to change a smooth curve point into a corner curve point.

WORKING IN COLOR 6

My first computer was a Macintosh SE which is currently serving as a bookend under my desk. It has a built-in screen that is even smaller than the pages of this book. The screen only displays black and white images.

Still I used it to create all sorts of full-color illustrations and designs. I just defined all my colors using numerical values and used my vivid imagination to visualize what the job would actually look like when it was finally printed.

I doubt you're using anything as primitive as my old computer. Today it's hard to find anyone who doesn't have a full-color monitor measuring 17 inches or more. (If you don't have a large monitor, my condolences.)

Interestingly, though, there are very few differences in the principles of working in color from the old days to now. In fact, the basics of working in color aren't computer specific; they come from years and years of print shops printing color images in documents.

Working with Color Modes

There are three different models for defining colors: CMYK, RGB, and LAB. Each model is used for different purposes.

You choose the color mode and mix colors in the Color palette.

To work with the Color palette:

1. If the Color palette is not visible, choose Window > Color to open the palette **❶**.

   or

   If the Color palette is behind other palettes, click the Color palette tab.

2. If the color sliders are not visible, choose Show Options from the Color palette submenu **❷**.

The CMYK color model is used primarily for print work. CMYK colors are mixed using representations of the four inks used in process printing: cyan, magenta, yellow, and black.

To mix CMYK colors:

1. Choose CMYK from the Color palette submenu. This opens the palette in the CMYK mode **❸**.

2. Choose one of the following methods to define the amount of cyan, magenta, yellow, or black ink in the color:

   • Type a value from 0 to 100 percent in the four color fields.

   • Drag the sliders for each of the four color fields.

   • Click a color in the CMYK spectrum area.

   TIP Click the solid white or black rectangles to the right of the spectrum to quickly get 100% black or white.

   TIP Hold the Shift key as you drag one slider to have the others move along with it.

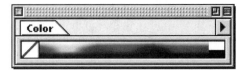

❶ The **Color palette** with the options turned off shows only the spectrum for choosing a color.

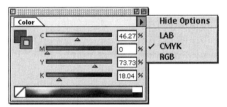

❷ The **Color palette submenu**.

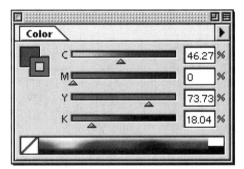

❸ The CMYK Color palette.

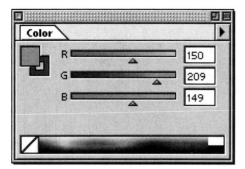

④ The **RGB Color palette** mixes color for onscreen display such as Web sites.

The RGB color model is used primarily for onscreen work such as presentations and web sites. The RGB colors—red, green, and blue—are mixed using representations of the three colors of light that blend together in television and computer monitor screens. You can create more vivid colors using RGB colors than with CMYK colors.

To mix RGB colors:

1. Choose RGB from the Color palette submenu **④**.

2. Choose one of the following methods to define the amount of red, green, or blue in the color:

   • Type the value from 0 to 255 in the three color fields.

   • Drag the sliders for each of the three color fields.

   • Click a color in the RGB spectrum area.

Working with Color Modes

The LAB color model defines colors according to a *luminence* (lightness) component, and two color components, *a* and *b*. The *a* component defines the green to red values. The *b* component defines the blue to yellow values. Unlike CMYK or RGB colors that can change depending on the type of monitor or printer they are sent to, LAB colors are designed to be device-independent so that the color does not change from one source to another.

TIP The proper name for LAB colors is L*a*b and is pronounced by spelling out the name (*el-ay-bee*), not by saying the word lab.

To mix LAB colors:

1. Choose LAB from the Color palette submenu ❺.

2. Choose one of the following methods to define the three components of the color:

   • Type the value from 0 to 100 in the L field or type the value from -128 to 127 in the A or B fields.

   • Drag the sliders for each of the three fields.

   • Click a color in the LAB spectrum area.

TIP The out-of-gamut symbol ❻ appears if you choose an RGB or LAB color that cannot be printed using process inks.

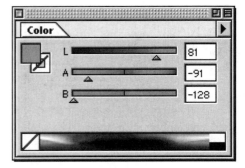

❺ The **LAB Color palette** mixes colors that look consistent no matter whether you print or display them onscreen.

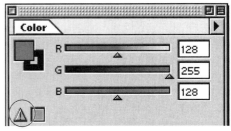

❻ The **out-of-gamut symbol** for RGB or LAB colors indicates the color shown on screen will not print the same using process color inks.

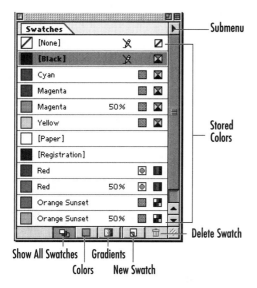

Submenu

Stored Colors

Delete Swatch

Show All Swatches | Gradients
Colors | New Swatch

❼ The **Swatches palette** shows all the saved colors.

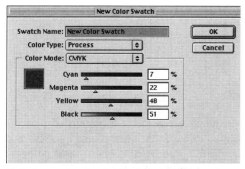

❽ Define new colors in the **New Color Swatch** dialog box.

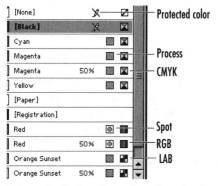

Protected color

Process

CMYK

Spot

RGB

LAB

❾ Icons in the Swatches palette show details about the stored colors.

Storing Colors

Colors mixed in the Color palette are temporary. As soon as you mix a new color, the old one is replaced. If you want to use a color again, you must add it to the Swatches palette.

To work with the Swatches palette:

1. If the Swatches palette is not visible, choose **Window > Swatches** to open the palette **❼**.

    or

    If the Swatches palette is behind other palettes, click the Swatches palette tab.

2. Click the Show All Swatches icon to see all the colors in the document.

To add a color to the Swatches palette:

1. Use the Color palette to define a color *(see page 94)*.

2. Choose New Color Swatch from the Swatches palette submenu. This opens the New Color Swatch dialog box **❽**.

3. Enter a name for the color in the Swatch Name field.

4. Choose Process or Spot from the Color Type pop-up list. *(For an explanation of the difference between process and spot colors, see "Process or Spot?" on page 98.)*

5. Use the Color Mode pop-up list to change the mode from the one originally defined in the Color palette.

6. Use the sliders to change the values from the ones originally defined.

7. Click OK to add the color to the Swatches palette **❾**.

You can also define and add colors directly in the Swatches palette (bypassing the Color palette). This makes it easy to define many colors at once.

To define colors in the Swatches palette:

1. Choose New Color Swatch from the Swatches palette submenu. This opens the New Color Swatch dialog box.

   or

   Hold the Option/Alt key as you click the New Swatch icon.

2. Name the color and set the other options as described in steps 4 through 7 of "To add a color to the Swatches palette" on the previous page.

Once you add a color to the Swatches palette, you can modify that color later.

To modify a color swatch:

1. Select the swatch and choose Swatch Options from the Swatch palette submenu. This opens the Swatch Options dialog box which is the same as the New Color Swatch dialog box (*see ❽ on the previous page*).

   or

   Double-click the swatch in the palette.

2. Make changes to the color.

   TIP The Swatch Options dialog box adds a Preview checkbox. Use it to see how the changes affect the colors applied to objects in the document.

3. Click OK to apply the changes.

Process or Spot?

Process colors are colors printed using small dots of the four process inks, cyan, magenta, yellow, and black. Spot colors are printed using special inks.

For example, if you look at the process color green printed in a magazine, that color is actually a combination of cyan and yellow printed together in a series of dots. However, a spot color green is printed by using actual green ink.

The benefit of spot colors is that you can exactly match a special color or use specialty colors such as fluorescents or metallics that could never be created using process inks. The benefit of process colors is that you can use just four inks to create thousands of different color combinations.

Once you create color swatches, you can apply them via the Fill and Stroke controls in the Toolbox or Color palette.

To apply a swatch color:

1. Create the object or text that you want to color.

2. Select either the Fill or Stroke icons in the Color palette or Toolbox. *(For more information on the Fill or Stroke icons see the figures in Chapter 4, "Working with Objects.")*

3. In the Swatches palette, click the color you want. This applies the swatch to the object.

If you define and store colors with a specific document open, those colors are stored in the Swatches palette only for that document. However, you can create colors that are available as the default colors for all new documents.

To create default colors:

1. Close all documents but leave InDesign running.

2. Use any of the methods in this section, "Storing Colors" to define and store a color in the Swatches palette. The color will appear in the Swatches palette of all new InDesign documents.

The Color Paper

The swatch labeled [Paper] in the Swatches palette allows you to change the background color of the pages in your document. This can be helpful if your document will be printed on colored paper, specialty paper, or even newsprint that is not completely white. You can modify the paper color to help judge how your images will look when printed.

Storing Colors

You can also delete colors from the Swatches palette.

To delete colors:

1. Select the color you want to delete.

To select a series of adjacent swatches, hold the Shift key and select the last swatch. This highlights all the swatches in between.

Hold the Command/Ctrl key to select non-adjacent swatches.

2. Click the Delete Swatch icon or choose Delete Swatch from the Swatches palette submenu.

3. If the swatch is used within the document, the Delete Swatch dialog box appears asking how you want to replace the deleted swatch ⑩:

- To swap the color with one from the Swatches palette, choose Defined Swatch and then pick a swatch from the pop-up list.

- To leave the color as an unnamed color applied to the object, choose Unnamed Swatch. *(For more information on unnamed colors, see page 104.)*

TIP The default swatches None, Paper, Black, and Registration cannot be deleted.

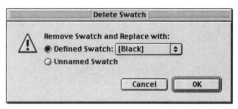

⑩ The **Delete Swatch** dialog box lets you choose how deleted swatches will be replaced in a document.

If you have many colors in your document that you are not using, you may want to delete them to avoid confusion when the file is sent to a print shop.

To delete all unused colors:

1. Choose Select All Unused in the Swatches palette submenu.

2. Click the Delete Swatch icon or use the Delete Swatch command in the Swatches submenu.

Sometimes it is easier to duplicate a swatch and then adjust it to a new color than it is to start from scratch.

To duplicate a swatch:

1. Select the swatch.

2. Do one of the following:

   • Choose Duplicate Swatch from the Swatches palette submenu.

   • Click the New Swatch icon.

   • Drag the swatch onto the New Swatch icon.

The Registration Color

"Registration" is a color that is set to print on all plates of a document. For instance, if your document will be printed using process colors, you might want to create a note or mark that should be seen on all four plates. Rather than make the note in a combination of cyan, magenta, yellow, and black, you can apply the color Registration to the text for the note. This prints the note on all four plates.

Storing Colors

Using Swatch Libraries

Rather than redefine colors for every new project, you can use the swatch libraries to import colors from other InDesign or Adobe Illustrator documents. You can also use the swatch libraries from professional color systems from companies such as Pantone or Trumatch.

To add colors from swatch libraries:

1. Choose **Window** > Swatch Libraries and then choose one of the ten libraries that ship with InDesign *(see "The Swatch Libraries")*. This opens the Swatches palette for that library.

2. Scroll through the palette to find the color you want to add to your document.

3. Double-click the color.

   or

   Select the color and choose Add To Swatches.

   TIP Choose **Window** > Swatch Libraries > **Other Library** to open color palettes from other InDesign documents (.indd and .indt) and Adobe Illustrator documents (.ai and .eps).

Many swatch libraries, such as those from Pantone, have numbers associated with each color. Instead of scrolling through a long list of colors, you can type the number of the color to go directly to it.

To choose swatches by numbers:

1. Hold Command-Option (Mac) or Ctrl-Alt (Win) and click inside the Swatches palette. A line appears around the inside of the palette **⓫**.

2. Type the number of the color. This selects the color.

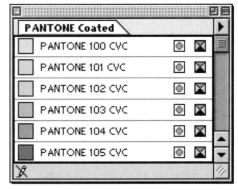

⓫ The black line around the inside of the palette indicates you can type the number to choose a color swatch.

The Swatch Libraries

Dicolor holds spot colors that can be matched in the DIC Color Guide.

Focoltone holds process colors. Color matching materials are available from Focoltone International, Ltd.

Pantone Coated contains spot colors. Pantone Process consists of process colors. Pantone Uncoated consists of the same spot colors as Coated, adjusted so they represent printing on uncoated paper. All Pantone colors can be matched to materials available from Pantone, Inc.

System (Macintosh) includes the colors of the Macintosh operating system.

System (Windows) includes the colors of the Windows operating system.

Toyo consists of spot colors. Color matching materials are available from the Toyo Ink Manufacturing Co., Ltd.

Trumatch provides process colors. Color matching materials are available from Trumatch, Inc.

Web consists of the 217 colors that are shared by both the Macintosh and Windows system colors.

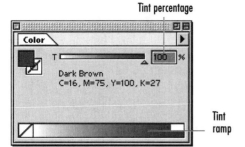

Tint percentage

Tint ramp

⓬ The Color palette for a **base color** chosen in the Swatches palette.

⓭ A base swatch and a 50% **tint swatch** for that base swatch.

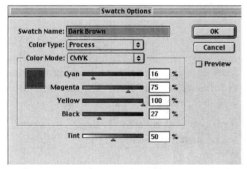

⓮ The Swatch Options for a tint.

Creating Tints

Tints are screened or lighter versions of colors. Tints are used to create variations of spot colors. You can also use tints to quickly create lighter versions of process colors.

To create a tint of a swatch:

1. In the Swatches palette, select the *base color,* that is, the color you want to tint.

2. In the Color palette, use the slider or click in the ramp to create a tint of the base color ⓬.

3. Click the New Swatch icon to create a swatch of the tint you defined.

TIP Tints appear in the Swatches palette with the same name as the base color but with the tint percentage listed ⓭.

To edit tints colors:

1. Double click the name of the tint swatch in the Swatches palette. This opens the Swatch Options dialog box for tints ⓮.

2. To change the tint value, adjust the tint slider at the bottom of the dialog box.

TIP You can also modify the sliders for the base color whenyou open the Swatch Options dialog box for a tint.

3. Click OK to apply the changes.

TIP Anytime you modify a base color, all tints of that color update automatically.

Creating Unnamed Colors

Unnamed colors are colors that are applied to objects directly from the Color palette instead of through the Swatches palette. It is not a good idea to create objects using unnamed colors. You may find it difficult to modify unnamed colors if they are scattered through a document. Your service bureau or print shop may also have problems working with unnamed colors.

In order to avoid unnamed colors, you should know how they are created.

To create unnamed colors:

1. With an object or text selected, use the Color palette to define a fill color. This applies the unnamed color to the fill of the object or text.

2. With an object or text selected, use the Color palette to define a stroke color. This applies the unnamed color to the stroke of the object or text.

Once you have unnamed colors in your document, you can still turn them into named swatches.

To name unnamed colors:

1. Select the object or text that has the unnamed color.

2. In the Color palette or Toolbox, select the Stroke or Fill icon depending on where the unnamed color has been applied.

3. Click the New Swatch icon or follow any of the other methods to define a color (*see page 97*).

TIP InDesign does not provide any way to search for unnamed colors.

Avoiding Unnamed Colors?

Why do I warn against creating unnamed colors? Why may your service bureau warn you not to use them?

Your job will most certainly print, even with unnamed colors. The problem comes when someone tries to check to make sure all your colors are defined correctly.

Because the unnamed colors don't appear in the Swatches palette, there is no way for someone to easily find the colors in your document. So the checker will have to search, page by page, to see if there are any unnamed colors.

So, although there is nothing actually wrong with unnamed colors, it is better to always use the Swatches palette to apply colors. That way you will not have unnamed colors in your document.

Color stop   Midpoint control

⑮ The **New Gradient Swatch** dialog box.

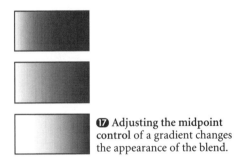

⑯ A **Linear gradient** changes colors along a line. A **Radial gradient** changes colors in a circular appearance.

⑰ Adjusting the **midpoint control** of a gradient changes the appearance of the blend.

Show All Swatches   Show Gradient Swatches

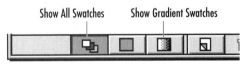

⑱ To see the gradients in the Swatches palette, click either the **Show All Swatches** or **Show Gradient Swatches** icon.

Creating Gradient Swatches

Gradients are blends that change from one color into another. InDesign creates gradients as swatches that can then be applied to objects.

To define a gradient:

1. Choose New Gradient Swatch from the Swatch palette submenu. The New Gradient Swatch dialog box appears **⑮**.

2. Enter a name for the gradient in the Swatch Name field.

3. Choose Linear or Radial in the Type field **⑯**.

4. Click one of the gradient stops on the Gradient Ramp to define a color in the gradient.

5. Choose the type of color for the selected stop from the Stop Color pop-up list.

   • Choose Named Color to choose one of the colors from the Swatch palette.

   • Choose LAB, CMYK, or RGB to define the stop color using unnamed colors. *(See "Avoiding Unnamed Colors?" on the previous page.)*

6. Click the other gradient stop to define a color for it.

7. Adjust the midpoint control to change the position where the two colors blend equally **⑰**.

8. Click OK to add the gradient to the Swatches palette.

TIP If you don't see the gradient listed in the Swatches palette, click either the Show All Swatches or Show Gradient Swatches icon at the bottom of the Swatches palette **⑱**.

Creating Gradient Swatches

To modify a gradient swatch:

1. Select the gradient swatch and choose Swatch Options from the Swatch palette submenu. This opens the Gradient Options dialog box which is the same as the New Gradient Swatch dialog box.

   or

   Double-click the gradient in the palette.

2. Adjust the midpoint, stop colors, or gradient type.

TIP The Gradient Options dialog box adds a Preview checkbox. Use it to see how the changes affect the gradients applied to objects in the document.

3. Click OK to apply the changes.

All gradients start with two colors; one at the start and the other at the end of the gradient ramp. However, you can easily add more colors to a gradient.

To add gradient color stops:

1. Open the New Gradient Swatch or Gradient Options dialog boxes.

2. Click the area below the gradient ramp. This adds a color stop to the ramp area **⓲**.

3. Make whatever changes you want to the color stop.

4. If necessary, move the color stop to a new position.

5. Click OK to apply the changes to the gradient swatch.

To delete a gradient color stop:

◆ Drag the color stop away from the ramp area and release the mouse. The gradient reblends according to the colors that remain.

TIP You cannot have fewer than two color stops in a gradient.

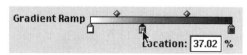

⓲ Adding a new color stop to the Gradient Ramp.

20 Click the **Gradient tool** in the Toolbox to control gradient fills in objects.

21 Drag the Gradient tool in the direction you want the gradient to blend.

You apply a gradient blend much as you would any swatch color.

To apply a gradient:

1. With the object or text selected, click either the Fill or Stroke icon in the Color palette or Toolbox.

TIP Text must be selected using the Text tool in order to apply a gradient to it.

2. Click the gradient swatch in the Swatches palette. This applies the gradient swatch to the object.

Once you apply a gradient, you can modify how the gradient spreads across the object.

To modify the spread of a gradient:

1. Select the object that has the gradient applied to it.

2. Click the Gradient tool in the Toolbox **20**.

3. Drag across the object with the Gradient tool to change the direction and the length of the gradient **21**.

Creating Gradient Swatches

Creating Unnamed Gradients

Just as you can create unnamed colors, you can also create unnamed gradients. These are gradients that are created only within the Gradient palette and are not stored in the Swatches palette. Again, like unnamed colors, it is not a good idea to work with unnamed gradients.

To create unnamed gradients:

1. If the Gradient palette is not visible, choose **Window** > **Gradient** to open the palette ㉒.

    or

    If the Gradient palette is behind other palettes, click the Gradient palette tab.

2. If you only see the gradient ramp, choose Show Options from the Gradient palette submenu to see all the controls in the palette.

    TIP If the color stops are not visible, click the area under the ramp to display the color stops in the Gradient palette.

3. Use the Type pop-up list to choose between Linear or Radial.

4. Select a color stop and adjust the sliders in the Color palette to define the color at that position.

    TIP You cannot use named colors in unnamed gradients.

5. Select the other color stop and use the sliders in the Color palette to define the color at that position.

6. Set the Angle of the gradient in the Angle field.

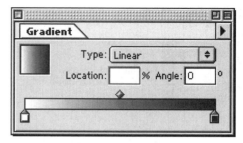

㉒ The Gradient palette.

㉓ The Gradient icon in the Toolbox.

The Gradient palette holds only one gradient at a time. Each unnamed gradient is maintained until you create another gradient.

To apply previously created unnamed gradients:

1. Select the object that you want to apply the gradient to.

2. Click the Gradient icon in the Toolbox **㉓**.

   or

   Click the Gradient preview in the Gradient palette.

To modify unnamed gradients:

1. Select the object with the unnamed gradient.

2. Make any changes to the gradient in the Gradient palette.

TIP If the object is not selected, the changes will not be applied to that gradient.

TIP The Gradient tool can be used to change the angle of unnamed gradients *(see page 107)*.

Creating Unnamed Gradients

Overprinting Colors

Overprinting is a technique that allows you to set the color of one object to mix with any colors underneath. For instance, without overprinting, a yellow object placed over a blue background will print as yellow. But with overprinting turned on, the yellow object mixes with the blue background to create green.

TIP You cannot see the effects of setting an object to overprint until you create film separations.

To set a fill or stroke to overprint:

1. Select the object.

2. If the Attributes palette is not visible, choose **Window** > **Attributes** to open the palette **24**.

   or

   If the Attributes palette is behind other palettes, click the Attributes palette tab.

3. Check Overprint Fill to set the object's fill color to overprint.

4. Check Overprint Stroke to set the object's stroke color to overprint.

24 The **Attributes palette** allows you to set the fill or a stroke to overprint.

IMPORTED GRAPHICS 7

One reason desktop publishing became so popular is how easy it is to combine graphics such as photographs and illustrations with type.

In the years before computers, specialized workers, working under the exotic name *strippers,* manually trimmed away the blank areas around graphics so that text could be placed around the image. (That's where they got the name stripper. They were combining strips of film together.)

It was even more complicated to get text to appear over an illustration. The image and text had to be combined by photography and then stripped into the layout.

With page layout programs such as InDesign it takes a few clicks of a mouse to combine type and artwork together. It's enough to make old-time strippers hang up their tassles!

Placing Artwork

Most artwork for InDesign comes from other sources. You can use scanners or digital cameras. Or the artwork can be created in the computer and saved using programs such as Adobe Photoshop, Adobe Illustrator, Macromedia FreeHand, or Adobe Acrobat.

Once you have created artwork, you can place it in InDesign documents. You can create frames and then place images into them, or you can create the frame automatically as you place the artwork.

To place artwork:

1. Choose **File**>**Place**. This opens the Place dialog box **①**.

2. Navigate to find the file you want to import. *(See "File Formats" on the next page for a list of the types of files you can place in InDesign.)*

3. Check Show Import Options to open the Import Options dialog box **②** before you place the file. *(See page 116 for more information on working with Import Options.)*

4. Click Choose to load the graphic into an image cursor **③**.

5. Click the image cursor to place the image in a frame the same size as the artwork.

   or

   Drag the image cursor to define a frame to hold the artwork.

TIP Only the frame is sized when you drag the image cursor. The artwork stays at its actual size. *(See page 121 for how to change the size of an image inside a frame.)*

TIP You can also place artwork into an existing frame.

TIP Hold the Shift key as you click Choose, to open the Import Options dialog box, even if the option is not checked.

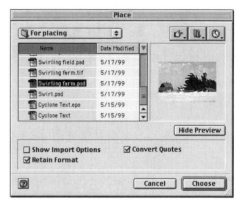

① The **Place** dialog box.

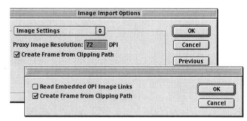

② The **Import Options** for two different types of files.

 ③ The **loaded image cursor** appears when you prepare to place artwork.

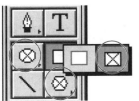

❹ The Graphic Frame **tools** make graphic frames of different shapes.

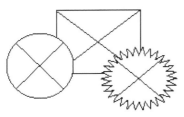

❺ The crossed lines designate **graphic frames.**

Making Graphic Frames

A frame can hold either text or a graphic. So if you have drawn an object frame or a text frame, you can still place a graphic in it. InDesign also lets you designate frames specifically for artwork.

TIP Use the graphic frames to indicate areas where only artwork, not text, should be placed.

To draw graphic frames:

1. Choose the Rectangle Frame tool, Ellipse Frame tool, or Polygon Frame tool from the Toolbox **❹**.

2. Draw a frame.

Crossed lines appear inside graphic frames **❺**. *(For more information on creating rectangles, ellipses, and polygons, see Chapter 4, "Working with Objects.")*

You can also convert any frame to a graphic frame.

To convert a frame to a graphic frame:

1. Select the frame you want to convert.

2. Choose **Object >Content >Graphic.** This converts the frame into a graphic frame and displays the crossed lines within the frame.

File Formats

There are a wide variety of graphic formats that can be added to InDesign documents:

Adobe Illustrator (AI)

Adobe Photoshop (PSD)

Encapsulated PostScript (EPS)

Desktop Color Separation (DCS)

Graphics Interchange Format (GIF)

Joint Photographer's Expert Group (JPEG)

Macintosh QuickDraw Picture (PICT)

PC Paintbrush (PCX)

Portable Document Format (PDF)

Portable Network Graphics (PNG)

PostScript (PS)

Scitex Continuous Tone (SCT)

Tagged Image File Format (TIFF)

Windows Bitmap (BMP)

Windows Metafile (WMF)

Making Graphic Frames

Special Frame Shapes

You can use the Pen tool *(see Chapter 5)* to draw the paths that create special frame shapes. You can also create special frame shapes by converting text to frames.

To convert text to frames:

1. Use the Selection tool to select the frame that contains the text.

   or

   Highlight the selected text within the frame.

2. Choose **Type** > **Create Outlines.** Each character of text is converted to a frame that can be modified and used to hold an imported graphic **❻**.

TIP The converted frames are combined as compound paths. Choose **Object** > **Compound Paths** > **Release** to color each individual frame or place different images in each frame. *(For more information on working with compound paths, see page 76.)*

TIP If you select only a portion of the text within the frame, the highlighted text is converted to inline graphics within the frame. *(For more information on working with inline graphics, see page 131.)*

❻ The **Create Outlines** command converts text into frames that can then be modified or used to hold images.

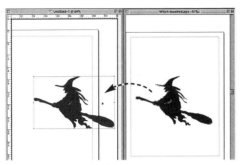

❼ Drag an image from a vector-drawing program into an InDesign document to convert it to an InDesign frame.

❽ Graphics converted to frames can hold images or text.

If you work with a vector-drawing program such as Macromedia FreeHand or Adobe Illustrator, you can also convert the paths in those programs to InDesign frames.

TIP This technique can be used with any program that copies paths using the AICB (Adobe Illustrator Clipboard).

To convert paths into frames:

1. Open the file in the vector-drawing program.

2. Select the paths.

3. Drag the paths from the vector-drawing program onto the window of the InDesign document.

4. When a black line appears around the InDesign window, release the mouse button. The paths are converted to InDesign unassigned frames ❼.

TIP Once the graphic has been converted to an InDesign frame, it can be used to hold an image or text ❽.

Special Frame Shapes

Setting Image Import Options

Just like the text import options, choices arise when you place graphics. Different types of graphics have different import options. If your image is a pixel-based image, such as a TIFF file, you have certain options. *(See the sidebar "Pixels or Vectors" on page 124.)*

To import pixel images:

1. Choose **File** > **Place** to open the Place dialog box.

2. Check Import Options.

3. Select a pixel-based image and then click Choose. This opens the Image Import Options dialog box for pixel-based images ❾.

4. Choose Image Settings from the pop-up list.

   • Set an amount in the Proxy Image Resolution field. The higher the value, the greater the detail displayed onscreen ❿.

   • If the image has a clipping path from a program such as Adobe Photoshop, you can choose Create Frame From Clipping Path. *(See the sidebar "Working with Clipping Paths" on the next page.)* This converts the path into a frame you can manipulate in InDesign ⓫.

5. Click OK to place the image.

TIP Proxy image settings are only applicable if you set the Image Display to Proxy Image in Preferences *(see page 240)*.

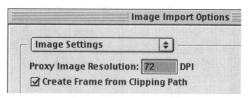

❾ The **Image Import Options** dialog box lets you set the import options for pixel-based graphics.

❿ The effect of setting different **proxy image resolutions.**

⓫ An embedded clipping path can be converted into a frame, which you can manipulate within InDesign.

☐ Read Embedded OPI Image Links
☑ Create Frame from Clipping Path

⑫ The EPS import settings.

You have different import options for EPS images.

To import EPS images:

1. Choose File > Place to open the Place dialog box.

2. Check Import Options.

3. Select an EPS file and then click Choose. This opens EPS import settings **⑫**.

4. Check Read Embedded OPI Image Links only if your service bureau has instructed you to have InDesign read the OPI links and perform the image swapping.

5. Check Create Frame From Clipping Path to convert the embedded path to a frame that you can manipulate in InDesign. *(See "Working with Clipping Paths" on this page.)*

TIP If the image does not have a clipping path you can create one within InDesign *(see page 129)*.

6. Click OK to place the image.

Working with Clipping Paths

All images created in pixel-based programs such as Adobe Photoshop must be rectangular. However, if you have a picture of an object against a background, you might want the background to be transparent.

A clipping path sets the boundary that designates which areas of an image should be seen and which ones should be transparent.

The clipping path can be drawn in Adobe Photoshop using a Pen tool very similar to the one in InDesign or by converting selections into paths. The clipping path command is then applied to the path.

When you bring the image into InDesign, any area outside the path is transparent.

Setting Image Import Options

InDesign also lets you place PDF files as graphics. The import options for PDF files are different from the other types of graphics.

To import PDF files:

1. Choose **File** > **Place** to open the Place dialog box.

2. Check Import Options.

3. Select a PDF file and then click Choose. This opens the Place PDF dialog box 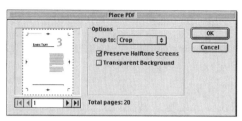.

4. Use the page selectors to select the page you want to place.

5. Use the Crop To pop-up list to determine how the PDF should be cropped within the frame. Choose one of the following options:

   - Content crops to the active elements of the page which includes pagemarks.

   - Art crops to the area defined as placeable art.

   - Crop crops the area that is displayed or printed by Acrobat.

   - Trim crops to the area that is the final trim size.

   - Bleed crops to the area that is the total size of the image if a bleed area has been specified.

   - Media crops to the page size of the original document.

6. Choose Preserve Halftone Screens to use any halftone screens specified within the PDF document.

7. Choose Transparent Background to show only the elements of the page without the opaque background 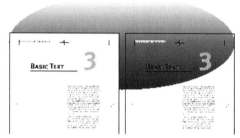.

TIP If you choose Transparent Background, you can make it opaque by setting a fill color to the frame containing the PDF *(see page 76).*

8. Click OK to place the image.

13 The **Place PDF** dialog box controls how PDF files are placed.

14 The effect of the **Transparent Background** on a placed PDF image.

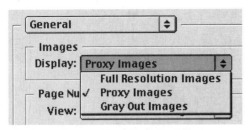

⓯ The Preferences dialog box allows you to set the display options for placed images.

⓰ The Gray Out Images option replaces an image with a gray area crisscrossed by lines.

Viewing Images

You can set placed images to display in different ways on the page. This lets you set how detailed the image appears or turn off the display entirely to speed the redraw of the page.

To set image previews:

1. Choose **File** > **Preferences** > **General** to open the Preferences dialog box **⓯**.

2. Choose one of the three options from the Images Display pop-up list.

   - Full Resolution Images displays images at the resolution of the image. For most professional print output this is 300 pixels per inch.

   - Proxy Images displays images at the proxy resolution that was created when the file was placed.

   - Gray Out Images displays a gray box instead of the actual image **⓰**.

   TIP Full Resolution provides the most detail but can slow screen redraw.

   TIP Gray Out creates the fastest screen redraw.

Viewing Images

Modifying Placed Images

After you place an image, you can still modify it on the page. You can modify both the frame and the image together, or just the graphic within the frame.

To modify the frame and the graphic:

1. Use the Selection tool to select both the frame and the graphic.

   A bounding box appears around the frame indicating that both it and the graphic are selected ⓱.

2. Choose any of the following to modify both the frame and the graphic:

   • Drag to move both the frame and the graphic.

   • Use any of the Transform palette fields *(see page 67)*.

   • Use the Rotate, Scale, or Skew tools *(see pages 65 and 66)*.

To modify the frame only:

1. Use the Direct Selection tool to select the edge of the frame.

   Four hollow anchor points appear on the corners of the frame indicating that only the frame is selected ⓲.

2. Choose any of the following to modify the frame only:

   • Drag an anchor point on the frame to change the shape of the frame.

   • Drag the edge of the frame to move it without moving the graphic ⓳.

   • Use any of the Transform palette fields.

   • Use the Rotate, Scale, or Skew tools.

⓱ The **bounding box** indicates both the frame and bounding box are selected.

⓲ The **hollow anchor points** indicate that only the frame is selected.

⓳ Drag the edge of a frame to move the frame without moving the placed graphic.

㉔ Drag artwork within a frame to move the artwork without moving the frame.

To modify the placed graphic only:

1. Use the Direct Selection tool to select the artwork within the frame.

   A bounding box for the placed artwork appears around the artwork.

2. Choose any of the following to modify the graphic only:

   • Drag the artwork to move it within the frame **㉔**.

   • Use any of the Transform palette fields.

   • Use the Rotate, Scale, or Skew tools.

Modifying Placed Images

Fitting Graphics in Frames

Several commands help you position and size artwork within frames.

To resize the graphic to the frame size:

1. Use the Selection tool to select both the frame and the graphic.

2. Choose **Object** > **Fitting** > **Fit Content to Frame.**

   This changes the size of the graphic to fit completely within the area of the frame **㉑**.

   TIP This command does not preserve the proportions of the artwork; the artwork may become distorted.

To proportionally resize to the frame size:

1. Use the Selection tool to select both the frame and the graphic.

2. Choose **Object** > **Fitting** > **Fit Content Proportionally.**

   This changes the size of the graphic to fit completely within the frame **㉒**.

To resize the frame to the graphic size:

1. Use the Selection tool to select both the frame and the graphic.

2. Choose **Object** > **Fitting** > **Fit Frame to Content.**

   This changes the size of the frame so that the artwork fits completely within the area of the frame **㉓**.

To center the graphic within the frame:

1. Use the Selection tool to select both the frame and the graphic.

2. Choose **Object** > **Fitting** > **Center Content to Frame.**

   This repositions the graphic so it is centered within the frame **㉔**.

㉑ The effect of the Fit Content to Frame command.

㉒ The effect of the Fit Content Proportionally command.

㉓ The effect of the Fit Frame to Content command.

㉔ The effect of the Center Content to Frame command.

㉕ When a frame is selected, choosing a fill color changes the background color of the frame.

㉖ When a placed image is selected, choosing a fill color changes the background color of the image.

Coloring Graphics in Frames

Once you have placed a graphic within a frame, you can employ a couple of techniques to change the color of the frame or the color of the image.

To color the frame background:

1. Use the Selection tool to select the both the frame and the graphic

   or

   Use the Direct Selection tool to select just the frame.

2. Choose the Fill icon in the Color palette or Toolbox.

3. Choose a color in the Swatches palette.

   The background color of the frame is visible wherever the image does not fill the frame **㉕**.

   TIP You can color a frame by choosing a color in the Color palette. However, this creates an unnamed color in the document and is not recommended.

If you import a grayscale TIFF, you can change the color of the image. This has the effect of colorizing the image. *(See "Colorizing Grayscale Images" on this page.)*

To color a grayscale image:

1. Use the Direct Selection tool to select the grayscale image.

2. Choose the Fill icon in the Color palette or Toolbox.

3. Choose a color in the Swatches palette.

   The grayscale image changes to a tint of the color chosen **㉖**.

   TIP Check with the service bureau, or the place that outputs your file if they have any problems with colorizing grayscale images.

Colorizing Grayscale Images

Your service bureau may instruct you not to colorize grayscale images. Or you may get a warning from a preflight program.

In theory there is nothing wrong with colorizing grayscale images, but individual production workflows may not be able to handle the images.

If you get a warning about grayscale images, check with the service bureau as to whether or not it can handle them.

Coloring Graphics in Frames

Linking Graphics

When you place an image, you do not actually place the image into the document. Only the screen preview of the image is incorporated as part of the file. In order to print the file, InDesign needs to access the original graphic. This is called a *link*.

TIP It is possible to link text files as well as graphics, but there are few practical advantages. *(See "Links for Text Files" on the next page.)*

To examine the links in a document:

1. Choose **File**>**Links.** This opens the Links palette **27**.

   The Links palette shows all the linked images in the document with their page numbers. Special symbols indicate the status of the image.

   - The Missing Link icon indicates that the original graphic is not in the same location as when it was placed.

   - The Modified Link icon indicates that the original graphic has been modified since it was placed.

2. Use the Links palette pop-up menu to choose one of the following to sort the list of graphics:

   - Sort By Name arranges the graphics in alphabetical order.

   - Sort By Status arranges the missing or modified graphics together.

   - Sort By Page arranges the graphics according to the page they are on.

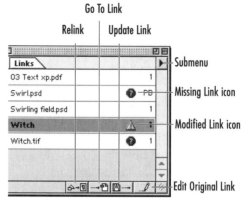

27 The **Links palette** lets you view and work with the linked images in a document.

Pixels or Vectors

There are two main types of graphics in desktop publishing. Pixel-based images (sometimes called *bitmapped,* or *raster* images) display images as a series of small rectangles. Scanners and digital cameras all capture images in pixels.

Vector images display artwork acording to paths filled with colors. They are the same as the vector shapes in InDesign. Programs such as Adobe Illustrator and Macromedia FreeHand create vector images.

Pixel-based images are usually used for photographs or images with blends. Vector images are usually used for more precise images such as maps or technical drawings.

One of the big benefits of working with vector images is that they can be scaled up or down without losing any details. Pixel-based images can lose details if they are scaled up too high.

28 The Missing or Modified Links notice appears when you open a file that has a missing link to a text or graphics file.

The Missing or Modified Links notice **28** appears when you open a file that has a missing link. You can then use the Links palette to relink the graphic.

To relink a missing graphic:

1. Select the missing link in the Links palette.

2. Click the Relink button. This opens the dialog box where you can navigate to find the missing file.

   or

   Choose Relink from the Links palette submenu.

3. Navigate to find the missing file.

4. Click OK to relink the graphic.

If a graphic has been modified, you can use the Links palette to update the link.

To update modified links:

1. Select the modified link in the Links palette.

2. Click the Update Link icon.

   or

   Choose Update Link from the Links palette submenu.

TIP You can select more than one link to update multiple graphics.

The Links palette also lets you move quickly to a specific graphic.

To jump to a linked graphic:

1. Select the link in the Links palette.

2. Click the Go To Link button.

   or

   Choose Go To Link from the Links palette submenu.

Linking Graphics

The Links palette can also be used to launch the application that created the file. This makes it easy to open and edit a graphic.

To edit a linked graphic:

1. Select the graphic you want to place.

2. Choose Edit Original from the Links palette submenu.

   or

   Click the Edit Original button in the Links palette.

   The graphic opens in the program that created it.

There is additional information you can learn about linked graphics.

To see the link information:

1. Select the linked graphic in the Links palette.

2. Choose Link Information from the Links palette submenu. This opens the Link Information dialog box ㉙.

   • Name shows the name of the file.

   • Date shows when the file was last saved.

   • Size shows the size of the file.

   • Page shows what page the file is on.

   • Edited indicates if the file has been modified since it was placed.

   • Link Needed shows if the file will be embedded in the document.

   • Color Space shows the type of color information in the file.

   • Profile shows what type of color management profile has been applied to the file.

   • File Type shows what program was used to save the file.

   • Location shows the complete path to find the file.

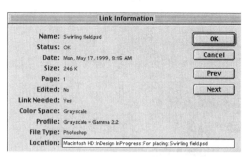

㉙ The **Link Information** dialog box gives you information about a placed graphics.

Embedding Graphics

Usually, only the preview of a graphic is contained within an InDesign file. You can, however, embed a graphic within the InDesign file. This means that all the information necessary to print the file is contained within the InDesign document.

To embed graphics:

1. Select the placed file.

2. Choose Embed from the Links palette submenu. A dialog box tells you the file size and asks if you want to embed the image.

3. Click Yes. The file name disappears from the Links palette.

TIP Use the same steps to embed text files within InDesign. Embedded text files do not add to the InDesign file size.

TIP If you copy or duplicate embedded graphics, each copy of duplicate adds to the file size.

TIP Once you have embedded a graphic, do not delete the original file from your hard disk or storage disks. InDesign does not have a command to unembed images.

When to Embed Graphics

You may be tempted to embed many, if not all, of your graphics within the InDesign document. After all, it makes it much easier to send a file to the service bureau if you don't have to remember to send the graphics along with it. *(For more information on preparing files for printing, see Chapter 12, "Output.")*

Embedding graphics increases the size of the InDesign file. Just a few large graphics can make the InDesign file quite large. This means the file will take a long time to open or save.

You may want to embed small graphics, such as logos. That's fine. But watch out especially if those files are on master pages. Every time an embedded graphic from a master page appears on a document page, it adds to the file size. So embedding a small logo can increase the file size dramatically if that logo is repeated on many pages.

My own feeling is to avoid embedding graphics. That way I don't have to worry about the file size.

Using Clipping Paths

Images from programs such as Adobe Photoshop are rectangular. If you want to see only part of the image you import, you can create a *clipping path* that surrounds the part of the image that you want to see. The rest of the image becomes transparent.

Once you have assigned a clipping path to a graphic, you can use the clipping path within an InDesign file. The most versatile file format for working with clipping paths is EPS, Encapsulated PostScript file. The EPS format allows you to import a file with a built-in clipping path.

⑳ An example of how a **clipping path** allows an image to have a transparent background.

To use an EPS with a clipping path:

1. Choose **File > Place** and select an EPS file with a clipping path.

2. In the Import Options dialog box, uncheck Create Frame From Clipping Path.

3. Place the image. The area outside the clipping path appears transparent **⑳**.

Unfortunately, you cannot edit the built-in clipping path of an EPS within InDesign. However, you can convert the clipping path to an InDesign frame, which you can edit using InDesign tools.

㉛ A clipping path converted to a frame can be modified within InDesign.

To convert a clipping path to a frame:

1. Choose **File > Place** and select a file that has been saved with a clipping path.

2. In the Import Options dialog box, check Create Frame From Clipping Path.

3. Place the image. The frame follows the shape of the clipping path.

4. Use the Direct Selection tool to modify the frame **㉛** if necessary.

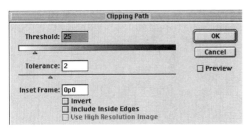

32 The **Clipping Path** dialog box allows you to create a clipping path from the difference between the dark and light colors an image.

33 An example of how the **Include Inside Edges** in a clipping path creates transparent areas within the foreground image like the circled area within the witch's hat.

What happens, though, if your image does not contain a clipping path? Fortunately, InDesign can create a clipping path frame from the differences between the dark and light colors of the image.

To create a clipping path:

1. Select the placed image.

2. Choose **Object** > **Clipping Path**. The Clipping Path dialog box appears **32**.

3. Adjust the Threshold slider to define the color that is used as the area outside the clipping path. 0 is pure white.

4. Adjust the Tolerance slider to allow a slight variation in the Threshold color. A high tolerance often smooths out small bumps in the path.

5. Type a value in the Inset Frame field to shrink the entire path into the image. A small inset value may help a clipping path follow the contours of the image better.

TIP A negative inset expands the path away from the image.

6. If necessary, check Invert to switch which areas the path makes visible and which areas are left transparent.

7. Check Include Inside Edges to add areas that are enclosed by the foreground image **33** to the clipping path.

8. Check Use High Resolution Image to have InDesign calculate the clipping path from the high resolution version of the file rather than the onscreen preview. This is a slower, but more accurate way of calculating the clipping path.

Using Clipping Paths

Nesting Elements

Once you have an image in a frame, you can then paste it into another frame. This is called *nesting elements*. This allows you to combine different types of images together. For instance, you can use nested elements to add a stroke to the frame around an image that contains a clipping path **34**.

To create a nested frame:

1. Select the element to be nested inside the frame.

TIP A nested element can be a graphic or text frame.

2. Cut or copy the element to the clipboard.

3. Draw a frame large enough to hold the nested frame.

4. Choose **Edit** > **Paste Into.** This places the element inside the frame.

TIP Frames can hold more than one level of nested frames.

TIP Use the Fit Content commands to position the nested frame *(see page 122).*

34 An image with a clipping path can be nested inside a stroked frame.

in case one of those great
whirlwinds arose,
mighty enoug
to crush any building in
its path. It was reached b

35 An **inline graphic** flows along with the text.

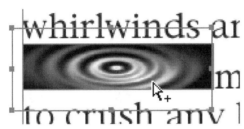

36 The **Group Selection** tool allows you to select multiple items within nested elements.

You can nest graphics within text frames to create inline graphics. Essentially you paste the graphic frame as a character into the text. Inline graphics make it easy to keep a graphic near a certain area of text.

To create an inline graphic:

1. Select the element that you want positioned.

2. Cut or copy the element to the clipboard.

3. Click to place an insertion point where you want the inline graphic to be positioned.

4. Choose **Edit** > **Paste**. The element is pasted into the text and flows along with any changes to the text **35**.

TIP Use the Selection tool to select and move inline graphics up or down on the baseline.

Some special techniques are required to select and move items that are part of nested elements.

To select and move nested elements:

1. Use the Direct Selection tool to select the first of the nested elements.

2. Hold the Option/Alt + Shift keys. This changes the Direct Selection tool to the Group Selection tool cursor **36**.

3. Continue to hold the modifier keys and select another of the nested elements.

4. Release the modifier keys and move the selected elements using the Direct Selection tool.

Nesting Elements

LONG DOCUMENTS

There are two types of page layout projects. There are short and single-page projects that designers spend hours and hours painstakingly crafting so that every element is exactly right—and then there are long documents.

Long documents are projects that are one-, two-, three-hundred or more pages such as books, manuals, or magazines. The designers who work on long documents don't have time to fuss with every single element. They need to automate as many page layout functions as possible. Of course, every element still needs to be exactly right!

How do you know when you're working on a long document? Simple, when you've been working so long that you've missed dinner and the end is nowhere in sight and you can't remember a time when you worked on something else— that's a long document!

Adding Blank Pages

The most obvious distinguishing characteristic of long documents is that they have many pages. InDesign gives you several ways to add pages to your document. The simplest way is to specify a certain number of pages before you start your document *(see page 18)*. You may, however, need to add pages after you have already started work on a document.

To add blank pages, you need to have the Pages palette visible.

To open the Pages palette:

- If the Pages palette is not visible, choose **Window** > **Pages** to open the palette ❶.

  or

  If the Pages palette is behind other palettes, click the Pages palette tab.

If you just need to add just a few pages, you can add them manually.

To manually add pages:

1. Click the New Page icon in the Pages palette to add a single page.

   or

   Drag a master page or a non-master page from the bottom of the Pages palette to the top, document area of the palette ❷. *(See page 141 for how to use master pages.)*

2. Repeat as many times until you have added all the pages you need.

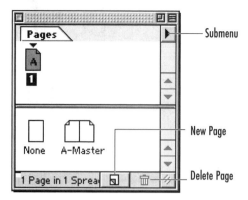

Submenu — New Page — Delete Page

❶ The Pages palette.

❷ Drag a master page from the bottom of the Pages palette to the document area to add pages to a document.

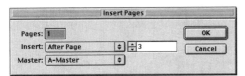

❸ The **Insert Pages** dialog box lets you add many pages at once to a document.

If you need to add many pages, you can add them automatically.

To automatically add pages:

1. Choose Insert Pages from the Pages palette submenu. The Insert Pages dialog box appears ❸.

2. Type the number of pages you want to insert in the Pages field.

3. Choose where to add the pages within the document from the Insert list:

   - Choose Before Page and then type a page number to insert the new pages before a certain page in the document.

   - Choose After Page and then type a page number to insert the new pages after a certain page in the document.

   - Choose At Start of Document to insert the new pages at the beginning of the document.

   - Choose At End of Document to insert the new pages at the end of the document.

4. Choose the master page that the new pages should be based on.

5. Click OK. The new pages appear in the Pages palette.

Working with Pages

Once you have many pages in your document, you need easy ways to navigate from one page to another.

To move to a specific page:

◆ Double-click the page in the Pages palette that you want to move to. This centers the page within the document window.

or

Double-click the name of the spread to fit both pages in the document window.

TIP You can also scroll or use the Hand tool to move through the document.

InDesign also lets you move from one page to another using the page controls at the bottom of the document window.

To use the window page controls:

◆ Click the window page controls ❹ to navigate through the document.

or

Enter a number in the Page field to move to a specific page.

TIP You can also navigate through the document by choosing the commands in the Layout menu.

To duplicate pages:

1. Select the page or spreads you want to duplicate.

2. Drag the pages onto the New Page icon.

or

Choose Duplicate Spread from the Pages palette submenu. This duplicates both single pages as well as spreads.

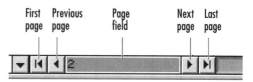

First page Previous page Page field Next page Last page

❹ The **window page controls** let you navigate through the document.

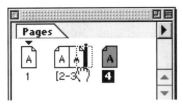

❺ The **black vertical line** indicates that the new page will be added to the island spread.

To delete pages:

1. Use the Pages palette to select the pages.

TIP Hold the Shift key to add contiguous pages. Hold the Command/Ctrl key to select noncontiguous pages.

2. Choose Delete Pages from the Pages palette submenu.

   or

   Drag the selected pages to the Delete Page icon at the bottom of the Pages palette.

3. When the confirmation dialog box appears, click OK to confirm your choice.

TIP Hold the Option/Alt key to bypass the confirmation dialog box.

Creating Island Spreads

Most documents are either single-page or facing-page documents. However, you can create spreads with more than one or two pages. These are *island spreads* like the fold-outs found in special issues of magazines.

To create an island spread:

1. Choose the page or pages in the document area that you want to designate as the island spread.

2. Choose Set as Island Spread from the submenu of the Pages palette. Brackets appear around the numbers of the pages indicating that the pages can have other pages added to the spread.

3. Move other pages in the document area next to the island spread.

4. Release the mouse when the black vertical line appears next to the island spread **❺**. This adds the page to the island spread.

Flowing Text

If you have a short amount of text, you can easily type the text directly in InDesign. However, if you are working with a long text, you most likely will import the text from a word processing program.

To import text from other sources:

1. Choose **File>Place**. This opens the Place dialog box **❻**.

2. Navigate to find the file you want to import.

3. Choose from the following options:

   • To keep any formatting applied to the text, click Retain Format.

   • To replace "dumb" (straight) quotes with "smart" (curly) ones, click Convert Quotes.

   • To open the specific import options for that type of text file, click Show Import Options **❼**.

4. Click Choose to load the text into a text cursor **❽**.

TIP If you hold the Shift key as you click Choose, you open the Import Options dialog box.

5. Drag the Loaded text cursor to create a text frame that contains the text. You can then link the text from one frame to another *(see page 56)*.

   or

   Click the Loaded text cursor inside an existing frame.

TIP The parentheses around the cursor indicates that the text will flow into that frame **❾**.

TIP To unload the text from the cursor, click any tool in the Toolbox.

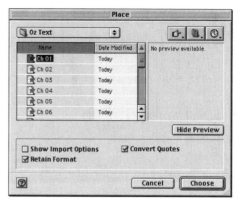

❻ The **Place** dialog box.

❼ The **Import Options** for two different types of text files.

❽ The **Loaded text cursor** for placing text.

❾ The Loaded text cursor inside a frame.

The **Semi-autoflow text cursor** indicates that the text will automatically load any overflow into the text cursor.

If the text you place is too long to fit in the frame, the overflow symbol appears. Rather than manually load the overflow text into a new frame you can use the Semi-autoflow command to easily load the cursor to create new text boxes to display the text.

To semi-autoflow text:

1. Place the text.

2. Hold the Option/Alt key to display the Semi-autoflow cursor ❿.

3. Click or drag to create a text frame. If there is more text in the story, the text is automatically loaded into the text cursor and is available to create another text box.

4. Hold the Option/Alt key and click or drag to create another text box linked to the first.

5. Repeat step 4 as many times as necessary to place all the text in the story.

TIP You can do any of the following without losing the text loaded in the cursor:

- Add pages.

- Zoom in or out.

- Scroll through the pages or document.

- Move palettes to new positions.

Flowing Text

Even the Semi-autoflow command may not be practical for flowing more than a few pages of text. You can automatically flow the text and create new pages at the same time using the autoflow feature.

To autoflow pages with text:

1. Use the Place command *(see page 138)* to load the text.

2. Hold the Shift key. This cursor changes to the Autoflow text cursor .

3. Click anywhere inside the margins of the page. This creates a text frame at that point that extends the width of the column. Additional text frames are created on new pages .

The text placed with the Autoflow command is contained within text frames that are added to the pages. InDesign also lets you flow text onto the frames that are on master pages. Importing text into those frames means that if you change the master page, the text frames adjust accordingly.

To flow text onto master page frames:

1. Click Master Text Frame in the New Document dialog box 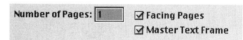. This creates an empty frame on each page of the document.

2. Use the Place command to load the text cursor.

3. Flow the text into the frame as follows:

   • Click inside the margins to flow the text onto that page only.

   • Hold the Option/Alt key to semi-autoflow the text onto that page only.

   • Hold the Shift key to autoflow the text and create as many pages as necessary.

⓫ The **Autoflow text cursor** indicates that the text will flow onto pages and create new pages as necessary.

⓬ The text frames created by the Autoflow command start at the point where the mouse was clicked. New text frames fill the entire area of the columns on the page.

⓭ The **Master Text Frame** option in the New Document dialog box.

Flowing Text

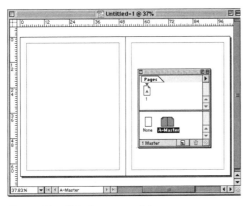

⓮ Double-click the name of the master page to view that **master page in the document window.**

Working with Master Pages

Master pages allow you to automate page layout changes. For instance, if you have a hundred-page book, you wouldn't want to have to draw a text frame on every page and type the name of the chapter or book title. Master pages allow you to place an object on the master page and have that object appear on all the document pages.

Every new document includes a master page. When you add objects to the master page, they appear on all the document pages based on that master page.

To add objects to a master page:

1. In the Pages palette, double-click the name of the default master page, A-Master. This opens the master page in the document window **⓮**.

2. Add text boxes, graphics, or any other elements you want on the master page.

   TIP If the document has been set for facing pages, there are two sides to the master page, left-hand and right-hand. The left-hand master page governs the left-hand document pages. Similarly the right-hand master page governs the right-hand document pages.

3. Double-click the name of the document page to make it the active page. Any items placed on the master page now appear on the document page.

   TIP Reopen the master page to make any changes to the master page elements. Those changes appear on the document pages.

Working with Master Pages

You can add master pages to a document. The allows you to have different layouts for different parts of your document.

To create new master pages:

1. Choose New Master from the Pages palette submenu. This opens the New Master dialog box **⑮**.

2. Choose a letter for the prefix for the master page.

TIP The prefix is the letter that appears inside the pages that have that master page applied to them.

3. Enter a name for the master.

4. Use the pop-up menu to set which master page, if any, the new master page should be based on.

TIP Basing one master page on another allows you to make changes on one master page that are applied to the other.

5. Enter the number of pages for the master. This allows you to create spreads with more than two pages **⑯**.

TIP To create a new master page without the New Master dialog box, hold the Command/Ctrl key and click the New Page icon at the bottom of the Pages palette.

As you work, you might want to convert a document page into a master page. InDesign makes it easy to turn a document page into a master page.

To convert a document page to a master page:

1. Select the page or pages.

2. Drag the page or pages from the document area down to the master page area **⑰**.

   or

   Choose Save as Master from the Pages palette submenu.

⑮ The **New Master** dialog box allows you to set the attributes for the master page.

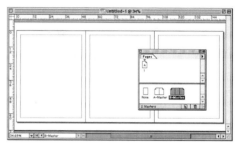

⑯ Set three or more pages to create **multi-page spreads**.

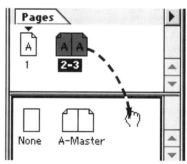

⑰ Drag a document page into the master page area to **convert the document page to a master.**

⓲ The Apply Master dialog box allows you to change the master that governs pages.

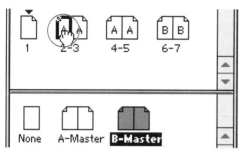

⓳ The rectangle around the single page indicates that the master will be applied to that page only.

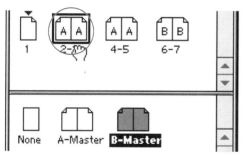

⓴ The rectangle around the spread indicates that the master will be applied to the spread.

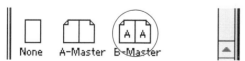

㉑ A letter inside the master page indicates that the master page is based on another.

The new pages you add to a document are based on the master page applied to the last page of the document. You can easily change the master page that governs pages.

To apply a new master to a page:

1. Select the page or pages.

2. Choose Apply Master to Pages from the Pages palette. This opens the Apply Master dialog box **⓲**.

3. Use the Apply Master pop-up list to apply a master to the pages.

4. Use the To Pages field to change the selected pages.

TIP The None page makes document pages that have no master page applied.

To apply masters with the Pages palette:

1. Drag the master page onto the document pages as follows:

   • To apply to a single page, drag onto the page. A rectangle appears around the page **⓳**.

   • To apply a spread, drag the master onto the spread. A rectangle appears around the spread **⓴**.

2. Release the mouse button to apply the master to the page.

You can also base one master page on another using the Pages palette.

To base masters on existing masters:

1. Drag the master page you want to govern onto the other master.

   • To base the spread on the master, drag the master onto the spread.

   • To base one page on the master, drag the master onto a single page.

2. Release the mouse button. The prefix of the master appears inside the second master page **㉑**.

Working with Master Pages

Adjusting Layouts

You certainly are not expected to set layouts perfectly the first time, every time. Fortunately, InDesign has a powerful layout adjustment feature that moves and resizes objects as you change the page size or margins.

Once layout adjustment is turned on, any changes to the layout change the position of the elements on both the master pages and document pages.

To set the layout adjustment options:

1. Choose Layout > Layout Adjustment. This opens the Layout Adjustment dialog box ㉒.

2. Set the options as follows:

   • Check Enable Layout Adjustment so that elements change when page size, orientation, margins, or columns are changed ㉓.

   • Set a value for the Snap Zone to specify how close an object must be before it will align and move to a margin or column guide, or page edge.

   • Check Allow Graphics and Groups to Resize so that elements change size as well as move during the adjustment.

   • Check Allow Ruler Guides to Move to have ruler guides move as part of the layout adjustment.

   • Check Ignore Ruler Guide Alignments to keep objects from moving along with ruler guides.

   • Check Ignore Object and Layer Locks to move objects that are locked or on locked layers.

3. Click OK to set the options.

   The document changes according to the new settings when the document setup or margins are changed.

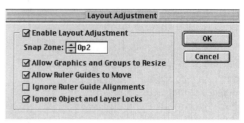

㉒ The **Layout Adjustment** dialog box turns on the automatic layout adjustment and controls the elements that change during layout adjustment.

㉓ The effect of changing the margins and page size when layout adjustment is turned on.

Ordinarily you modify the elements of a master page only on the master page itself. However, you can change master page elements on the individual document pages.

To modify master elements on document pages:

1. Move to the document page.

2. Hold Command-Shift (Mac) or Ctrl-Shift (Win) and click the element you want to modify. This selects the element.

3. Make any changes to the element.

TIP If you modify master page elements on a document page, the element may not change if you make changes to the master element.

For instance, if you add a stroke to an element you won't be able to change the element's stroke on the master page. The stroke of the element on the document page is removed from the control of the stroke of the element on the master page.

You can also hide master page items on document pages.

To change the display of master page items:

◆ Choose View > Display Master Items.

The master page items on that page are hidden and do not print.

How Many Master Pages?

While it may seem like a lot of work to set up master pages, the more masters you have the easier it is to lay out complicated documents.

A weekly magazine can easily have fifty or more master pages—some for the different editorial spreads and others for the different types of advertising spaces.

Some publications insist that every page be based on a master and do not allow any modifications of the master page elements. Others let the designers apply the master pages as a start for the finished document design.

You decide which way suits your work habits and the project.

Adjusting Layouts

Adding Page Numbers

The most common element that is added to a master page is the page-number character.

To add automatic page numbering:

1. Move to the master page.

2. Draw a text frame where you want the page number to appear.

3. Choose **Layout** > **Insert Page Number.** This inserts a special character in the text frame. The character appears as a page number on the document pages **㉔**.

4. If the master page is a facing-page master, repeat step 3 for the other side of the master page.

You may want to change how page numbers are displayed or the number they start from. You do that by creating a new *section* for the document.

To create a document section:

1. Move to the page where you want the section to start.

2. Choose Sections Options from the Pages palette submenu. The Section Options dialog box appears **㉕**.

3. Check Start Section to open the options.

4. Type the label (up to five characters) for the section in the Section Prefix field.

5. Use the Style pop-up list **㉖** to set the format for the numbering.

6. Choose between the two Page Numbering options:

   • Choose Continue From Previous Section to continue the number count from the previous pages.

   • Choose Start At and enter a number to start from a specific number.

7. Enter a label for the Section Marker. *(See the steps on the next page for how to work with the Section Marker.)*

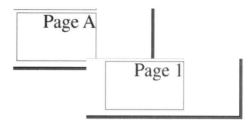

㉔ The **Auto Page Number character** appears as a letter on the master page but as a number on the document pages.

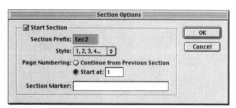

㉕ The **Sections Options** dialog box allows you to change the formatting and numbering of pages.

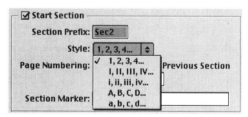

㉖ The **Style** pop-up list allows you to choose different formats for page numbering of a section.

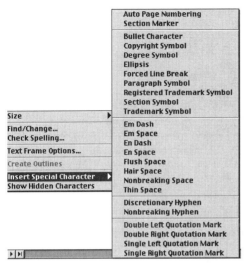

㉗ The context sensitive menu for **inserting items** into a text frame.

The Section Marker allows you to insert automatic custom labels for pages.

To add a Section Marker to pages:

1. Open the master page for the pages.

2. Place the insertion point in a text frame where you want the section marker to appear.

3. Right-click (Win) or Control-click (Mac) to display the context sensitive menu **㉗**.

4. Choose **Insert Special Character > Section Marker.** This adds the word Section inside the text frame on the master page.

5. Move to the document page to see the custom label in the text frame **㉘**.

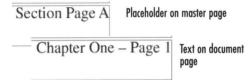

㉘ A **Section Marker** allows you to create custom labels for pages.

Using Layers

Layers can be helpful in working with intricate documents. For instance, if you have English and French versions of a document, you can put the text for each language on its own layer. You can then display just one version at a time.

To create new layers:

1. If the Layers palette is not visible, choose **Window** >**Layers** to open the palette ㉙.

2. Choose New Layer from the Layers palette submenu. This opens the New Layer dialog box ㉚.

   or

   Click the New Layer icon. This creates a new layer without opening the New Layer dialog box.

   TIP Hold the Option/Alt key as you click the New Layer icon to open the New Layer dialog box.

   TIP Double-click the name of a layer to open the Layer Options dialog box.

3. Name the layer and use the Color pop-up list to set a color for the layer.

   TIP The layer color is the color used to highlight the object frames and paths.

4. Click any of the frame options to do the following:

   • Show Layer makes the layer visible.

   • Show Guides displays the guides for that layer.

   • Lock Layer protects any objects on the layer from being changed.

   • Lock Guides protects any guides on the layer from being changed.

5. Click OK to create the layer.

Visible

㉙ The **Layers palette** allows you to add and delete layers as well as control the display of layers.

㉚ The **New Layer** dialog box allows you to set the name and other options for a layer.

Using Layers

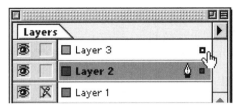

❸❶ Drag the object square in the Layers palette to move an object from one layer to another.

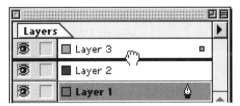

❸❷ Drag a layer between two others to change the position of that layer.

Once you have layers in your document, you can move objects onto the layers.

To apply objects to layers:

◆ Click the layer so that it is highlighted, and then create the object.

or

Select the object and then drag the object square in the Layers palette from one layer to another **❸❶**.

To reorder layers:

◆ Drag one layer above or below another to change the order that objects appear in the document **❸❷**.

The Layers palette submenu has many commands for working with layers.

To use the Layers palette submenu:

◆ Use the following commands within the Layers palette submenu:

• Layers Options for "Name of Layer" changes the options for the layer.

• Hide Others hides all the layers except the selected layer.

• Unlock All Layers unlocks all the layers in the document.

• Paste Remembers Layers sets the document so that objects are always copied and pasted onto their original layer. This applies within a document as well as to new documents.

• Delete Unused Layers deletes all layers that contain no objects.

Using Layers

You may want to combine the contents of one layer into another. This is called *merging* layers.

To merge layers:

1. Select the layers you want to merge.

2. Choose Merge Layers from the Layers palette submenu. All the objects on the layers are combined onto one layer.

TIP Unlike Photoshop, where the merge command reduces the file size, there is no change in the file size when merging layers in InDesign.

You can also use many of the Layers palette features to duplicate and reorder layers.

To use the Layers palette icons:

*   Use the following features within the Layers palette:

    *   Click the eyeball for a layer to show or hide the layer.

    *   Click the lock square for a layer to protect the layer from changes.

    *   Drag a layer up or down to change the order of the layers.

    *   Drag a layer onto the New Layer icon to duplicate the layer and its contents.

    *   Drag a layer onto the Delete Layer icon to delete the layer and its contents.

    *   Double-click the name of a layer to open the options dialog box for that layer.

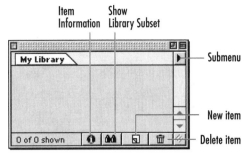

Item Information   Show Library Subset

Submenu

New item

Delete item

③③ A new library appears as a floating palette.

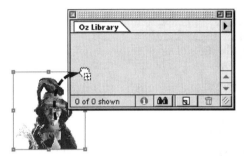

③④ Items can be dragged from the document into a library.

Working with Libraries

Another important utility for working with long documents, is the library feature. A library allows you to store elements, such as text frames or image frames. When elements are in a library, they can be dragged easily into open documents.

To create a library:

1. Choose Window > Libraries > New. This opens the New Library dialog box.

2. Use this dialog box to name the library file and select its location.

TIP The name of the library file appears in the tab of the Library palette.

3. Click Save. The library appears as a floating palette **③③**.

To add items to a library:

1. With a library open, select the item you want to insert in the library.

2. Click the New Library Item icon at the bottom of the Library palette.

   or

   Drag the item into the library **③④**. The item appears in the Library palette.

   or

   Choose Add Item from the Library palette submenu.

You can also add all the items on a page.

To add a page to a library:

1. With a library open, move to the page you want to add to the library.

2. Choose Add All Items on Page from the Library palette submenu.

TIP The Add All Items on Page command automatically labels the entry as a page in the library Item Information dialog box (see page 153).

Libraries can be opened and the elements in the libraries dragged onto any InDesign documents.

To add library items to a document:

1. Select the item in the library.

2. Drag the items from the library onto the page **35**.

   or

   Choose Place Item(s) from the Library palette submenu.

TIP Shift click to select and place more than one library item at a time.

To delete items from a library:

1. Select the item in the library.

2. Drag the item into the Delete Library Item icon.

   or

   Choose Delete Item(s) from the Library palette submenu.

3. A dialog box appears asking for confirmation that you want to delete the items. Click Yes.

TIP Hold the Opt/Alt key to bypass the dialog box when you delete a library item.

If you have many items in a library, you may want to change how the library items are displayed.

To change the library display:

♦ Choose List View to see the item name and an icon that indicates the type of item **36**.

   or

   Choose Thumbnail view to see the name and a small preview of the item **37**.

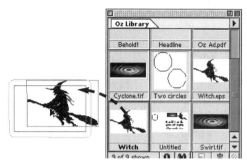

35 Items can be dragged from a library onto a document.

36 The List View shows the name of the items and an icon that shows the type of item.

37 The Thumbnail View shows the name of the items and a preview of the item.

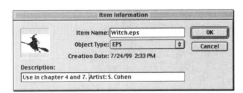

㊳ The Item Information **dialog box** lets you change the information assigned to each item.

You can also add information that makes it easy to search for library entries.

To add to the library information:

1. Select the item.

2. Click the Library Item Information icon.

   or

   Choose Item Information from the Library palette submenu. This opens the Item Information dialog box **㊳**.

3. Enter the name for the item in the Item Name field.

4. Use the Object Type pop-up list to choose the following categories:

   • Image describes InDesign frames that contain placed images, such as TIFF files.

   • EPS describes InDesign frames that contain placed EPS files.

   • PDF describes InDesign frames that contain placed PDF files.

   • Geometry describes InDesign frames and rules that do not contain images or text.

   • Page describes elements that compose an entire InDesign page.

   • Text describes InDesign frames that contain text.

TIP InDesign automatically assigns a category when items are entered into the library. You can change that listing to any category you want.

5. Enter a description for the item.

TIP The description can be keywords or other information that can help you identify the item.

Working with Libraries

Organizing Libraries

InDesign has a powerful search feature that makes it easy to locate specific items.

To search within a library:

1. Click the Show Library Subset icon.

    or

    Choose Subset from the Library palette submenu. The opens the Subset dialog box **39**.

2. Choose Search Entire Library to search all the entries in the library.

    or

    Choose Search Currently Shown Items to search through only those items currently displayed in the library.

3. Use the Parameters pop-up list and fields to set the criteria.

4. Click More Choices to add up to five choices to the parameters list.

5. Choose Match All to choose only those items that match all the search parameters.

    or

    Choose Match Any One to find items that meet at least one of the search parameters.

6. Click OK to display the items that meet the search criteria.

TIP Use the Back or Forward buttons to move to previous search settings in the Subset dialog box.

To display all the Library entries:

♦ Choose Show All from the Library palette submenu.

39 The **Subset dialog box** lets you find specific library items.

To sort library entries:

◆ Choose the Sort Items options from the Library palette submenu:

- By Name arranges the items in alphabetical order.

- By Oldest arranges the items in the order they were added with the oldest items first.

- By Newest arranges the items with the newest items first.

- By Type arranges the items in groups according to their categories *(see page 153)*.

Organizing Libraries

AUTOMATING TEXT 9

Just as there are special features for automating the layout of a document, there are also special features for automating text formatting. For instance, let's say I decided that every time I mentioned the program InDesign that it should be written in italic, as *InDesign.*

Do you think I would scroll through page after page looking for the word InDesign and then applying the italic version of the typeface one word at a time? Well, perhaps if I were being paid by the hour I might want to do that; but I'm not. So I would much rather finish the layout of this book as quickly and efficiently as possible.

That's what text automation features such as find and change, spelling check, and styles are designed for. Whenever a task threatens to become a laborious job of searching through an entire document or repeating the same commands over and over, most likely there's a special feature designed to automate the process.

Setting Tabs

One of the simplest, yet most useful, automation features is tabs. Tabs allow you to quickly line up columns of tabular material.

There are two parts to working with tabs. The first part is to type in the *tab characters* that force the text to jump to a certain position.

To enter tab characters:

1. Position the insertion point where you want the tab character to be.

2. Press the tab key on the keyboard. This creates a tab character in the text ❶.

TIP Choose **Type > Show Hidden Characters** to see the display of the tab character within the text *(see page 55)*.

TIP Do not insert more than one tab character for each column entry.

TIP InDesign recognizes the tab characters in imported text.

Frank » Writer

❶ A **tab character** is displayed as part of the hidden characters in text. Here, a tab separates the two words.

Setting Tabs

Position field   Magnet

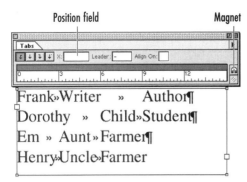

❷ The **Tabs ruler** lets you set the tab stops for text.

Left Center Right Decimal

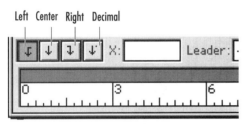

❸ The four **tab alignment icons.**

Right Left   Center   Decimal

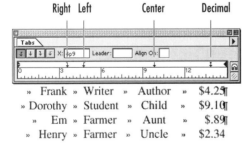

❹ Examples of how the **four tab alignments** control the text.

The second part to working with tabs is to set the *tab stops* or the formatting controls that set where the text should stop after it is forced to jump to a new position.

To set tab stops:

1. Select the text.

2. Choose **Text >Tabs.** The Tabs palette appears above the text frame ❷.

TIP If the Tabs palette is not positioned above the text, click the Magnet icon in the palette to automatically move the palette to the correct position.

3. Choose the type of tab alignment from the four tab icons in the ruler ❸. The four alignments work as follows:

   - Left aligns the left side of the text at the tab stop ❹.

   - Center centers the text around the tab stop ❹.

   - Right aligns the right side of the text at the tab stop ❹.

   - Align to Decimal aligns the text at the decimal point or period of the text ❹.

4. Click the ruler area where you want the tab stop to be positioned.

   or

   Type a number in the Position field.

   A small tab arrow appears that indicates the position of the tab stop.

TIP The default tab stops for all text are left-aligned tabs every half inch. Adding tab stops to the ruler overrides all tab stops to the left of the new tab.

TIP The Tabs palette can be kept onscreen like any other palette.

TIP Click the Magnet icon to align the Tabs palette to the top of the frame.

To change tab settings:

1. Select the text.

2. Open the Tabs palette.

3. To change the alignment of a tab stop, select the tab arrow and then click a new alignment icon.

4. To change the position of a tab stop, drag the tab arrow to a new position.

5. To delete a tab stop, drag the tab arrow off the area above the ruler.

TIP To clear all the tab stops from the rulers, choose Clear All from the Tabs palette submenu.

Many times you will want to have tab stops repeated at the same interval. InDesign makes it easy to set repeating tabs.

To set a repeating tab:

1. Position the first tab stop on the ruler.

2. With the tab stop still selected, choose Repeat Tab from the Tabs palette submenu. This adds new tab stops at the same interval along the ruler **⑤**.

TIP The tab stops created by the Repeat Tab command are not linked and move independently.

The Decimal tab aligns numerical data to a decimal point. However, you may need to align text to a different character. For instance, some European currency uses a comma instead of a decimal. InDesign lets you set a custom alignment character **⑥**.

To set a custom alignment character:

1. Choose the Decimal tab icon.

2. Add a tab stop to the ruler.

3. Replace the period in the Align On field with a different character.

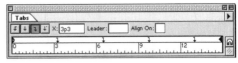

⑤ The **Repeat tab** command allows you to easily add tab stops at the same interval along the ruler.

Align On field

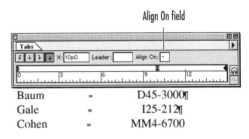

Baum	»	D45-3000¶
Gale	»	I25-212¶
Cohen	»	MM4-6700

⑥ How a **custom alignment character** allows text to align. Here the employee numbers align to the hyphen.

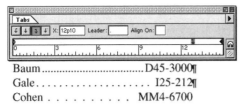

Baum .... D45-3000¶
Gale .... I25-212¶
Cohen MM4-6700

❼ An example of adding spaces to the tab leader field.

A *tab leader* allows you to automatically fill the space between the tabbed material with a repeating character. Tab leaders are often used in the tables of contents of books *(such as the table of contents in this book)*.

TIP Tab leaders are added when the reader needs to move along a wide column from one entry to another. The tab leader helps the reader's eye stay on the correct line of text.

To add tab leaders:

1. Select the tab stop arrow on the Tabs palette ruler.

2. Type up to eight characters in the Leader field.

TIP Press the tab key on the keyboard to preview the characters in the Leader field.

TIP Add spaces to the Leader field to add space between the leader characters ❼.

TIP You can select the characters in a tab leader like ordinary text and change the point size, kerning, or other attributes.

Setting Tabs

Checking Spelling

One of the most popular features of page layout programs is the Spelling Checker that chex a doccument for misspelt wordz.

To use the spell check command:

1. To check the spelling in a specific text frame or linked frames, click to place an insertion point within the text.

2. Choose **Edit** > **Check Spelling**. The Check Spelling dialog box appears ❽.

3. In the Search pop-up list, choose where the spelling check should be performed:

   - Document checks the entire document.

   - All Documents checks all open documents.

   - Story checks all the linked frames of the selected text.

   - To End of Story checks from the insertion point.

   - Selection checks only the selected text.

4. Click Start to begin the spelling check. InDesign searches through the text and stops and displays each error it finds.

TIP InDesign displays words not in its dictionary, duplicate words, or capitalization errors.

TIP The spelling checker does not find errors if they are reel (!!!) words.

The spelling checker may display a word that is correctly spelled. In that case you want to ignore the spelling checker.

To ignore the spelling checker:

◆ Click Ignore to continue the check without changing that instance of the text.

   or

   Click Ignore All to continue the spell check without changing any instance of that text.

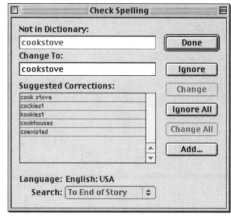

❽ The **Check Spelling** dialog box allows you to set the controls for the spelling check.

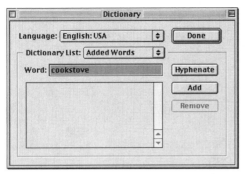

⍟ The **Dictionary** dialog box allows you to add or remove words from the dictionary used during a spell check.

To correct the error displayed:

1. Select a word from the Suggested Corrections list.

   or

   Type a correction in the Change To box.

2. Click Change to change only that instance of the word in the text.

   or

   Click Change All to change all instances of the word in the text.

To add words to the dictionary:

◆ Click Add when the word is displayed during the spelling check.

To edit the dictionary:

1. Choose **Edit** > **Edit Dictionary** to open the Dictionary dialog box **⍟**.

2. Choose the language from the Language pop-up list.

3. Choose Added Words or Removed Words from the Dictionary List.

4. Type the word you want to add in the Word field.

   or

   Click the word you want to remove.

5. Click the Add or Remove button.

TIP You can also control the hyphenation of the words in the dictionary. *(For more information on working with hyphenation, see Chapter 10, "Advanced Text.")*

Checking Spelling

Finding and Changing Text

InDesign has a powerful Find/Change command that lets you find all instances of text or formatting and make changes to the found items. The simplest Find/Change commands look for certain characters of text, called *text strings,* and changes them. For instance, you can change *Sept.* into *September.*

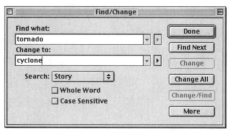

⑩ The Find/Change dialog box allows you to set the controls for searching for and replacing text.

To set the Find/Change text strings:

1. To find and change within a specific text frame or linked frames, click to place an insertion point within the text.

2. Choose **Edit > Find/Change.** The Find/Change dialog box appears **⑩**.

3. In the Search pop-up list, choose where the search should be performed:

   • Document checks the entire document.

   • All Documents checks all open documents.

   • Story checks all the linked frames of the selected text.

   • To End of Story checks from the insertion point.

   • Selection checks only the selected text.

4. In the Find What field, type or paste the text you want to search for.

5. In the Change To field, type or paste the text to be inserted.

6. Select Case Sensitive to limit the search to text with the same capitalization. For instance, a case-sensitive search for InDesign does not find Indesign.

7. Select Whole Word to disregard the text if it is contained within another word. For instance, a whole-word search for Design omits the instance in InDesign.

8. Click Start. InDesign looks through the text and selects each matching text string it finds.

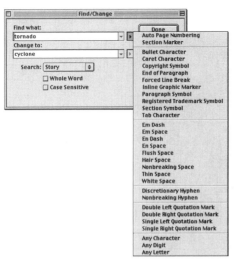

⓫ The **metacharacters menu** for the Find What field.

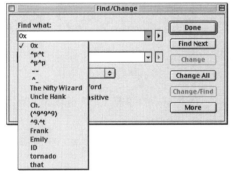

⓬ InDesign keeps a record of the past 15 text strings in the Find What or Change To fields.

As you run a Find/Change operation, you can choose whether or not to apply the changes.

To apply the Find/Change changes:

◆ Click Change to change the text without moving to the next instance.

or

Click Change/Find to change the text and move to the next instance.

or

Click Change All to change all the instances in the text.

You can tell InDesign to ignore or skip the change of a Find/Change instance.

To ignore a Find/Change instance:

◆ Click Find Next to avoid changing that instance of the found text and skip to the next occurrence.

InDesign also lets you search for special characters such as spaces, hyphens, paragraph returns, tab characters, or inline graphic markers. These are called *metacharacters* for the Find/Change commands.

To Find/Change metacharacters:

1. Choose the character you want to look for in the Find What pop-up menu ⓫.

2. Choose the character you want to substitute in the Change To pop-up menu.

3. Apply the Find/Change commands as described on the previous page.

TIP InDesign also keeps a list of the past 15 text strings for both the Find What and the Change To fields. You can use that list to quickly reapply searches ⓬.

The Find What list has three special meta-characters called *wildcard* characters. The wildcard characters allow you to search for items that you do not know the specific characters for.

To search for wildcard characters:

1. Choose one of the wildcard characters from the Find What pop-up list:

   • Any Character finds any character including spaces, tabs, returns, or text.

   • Any Digit searches for any number (0–9).

   • Any Letter searches for any alphabetical letter (a–z).

2. Set the Change To options.

3. Run the search.

TIP You can only use wildcard characters in the Find What field. *(See the sidebar on this page for a description of how to search using wildcard characters.)*

Working with Wildcard Characters

You cannot insert wildcard characters in the Change To field. However, that should not discourage you from working with wildcard characters.

The numbers for the steps of this book are an example of how I can format using wildcard characters. In the Find What field I enter ^9.^t, which is the code for any digit followed by a period and a tab.

I set the formatting for the number style in the Change To field. InDesign searches for any number followed by a period and a tab and applies the proper formatting.

In addition to text strings, you can also Find/Change formatting. This helps when making changes to text imported from word processing programs.

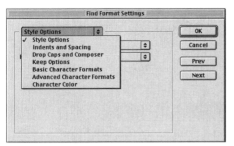

The **formatting options** for the Find/Change searches.

To Find/Change formatting:

1. Click More in the Find/Change dialog box. This opens the additional options for searches .

2. Click Format to open the Find Format Settings dialog box. Choose options from the pop-up menu or click Prev (previous) or Next.

   • Style Options changes character and paragraph styles. *(See the next page for information on working with styles.)*

   • Indents and Spacing searches for alignment, indents, and paragraph spacing.

   • Drop Caps and Composer searches for Drop Caps and Composer settings.

   • Keep Options changes the Keep With Next paragraph formatting.

   • Basic Character Formatting changes the character formatting options.

   • Advanced Character Formatting searches for the distortion formatting.

   • Character Color searches for colors from the Swatch palette.

3. Click OK. The search criteria are displayed in the Find Style Settings area.

   TIP Leave the Find What or Change To field blank to affect formatting no matter what the text.

4. Click Format to open the Change Format Settings dialog box. Choose options from the pop-up menu or click Prev or Next.

5. Click Find Next to make the changes.

   TIP Click Less to reduce the size of the Find/Change box so you can see the selected text in the document.

   TIP Click Clear to delete all the formatting in the Find or Change Style Settings areas.

Finding and Changing Text

Defining Styles

Styles are the most powerful feature for applying formatting. InDesign has two types of styles. *Paragraph styles* apply formatting for both character and paragraph attributes. *Character styles* apply formatting for only character attributes. *(For more information on working with character and paragraph attributes, see Chapter 3, "Text.")*

You can use the Paragraph Styles palette to define new paragraph styles for a document. *(See the sidebar on the next page for a description of how many styles a document needs.)*

To define a paragraph style manually:

1. Choose **Type** > **Paragraph Styles**. This opens the Paragraph Styles palette ⓮.

2. Choose New Style from the Paragraph Styles palette submenu. This opens the New Paragraph Style dialog box ⓯.

3. Name the new style.

4. Set the Next Style, Based On, and Shortcuts as described on pages 169 and 171.

5. Use the pop-up menu to set the paragraph and character attributes ⓰.

TIP If you need to reset one of the dialog boxes, hold the Option/Alt key. This changes the Cancel button to Reset which allows you to reset that one dialog box without losing settings in the other panels.

6. Click OK to define the style. The name of the style appears in the Paragraph Styles palette.

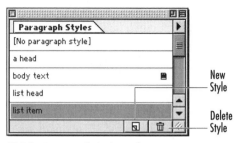

⓮ The **Paragraph Styles** palette.

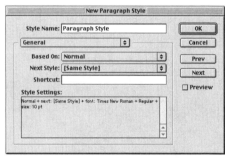

⓯ The **New Paragraph Style** dialog box is where you can name and define paragraph styles.

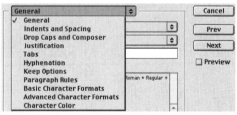

⓰ The **paragraph and character attributes** in the styles pop-up menu allow you to set all the attributes for a paragraph style.

Defining Styles

The easier way to define a style is to format the text and define the style by example.

To define a paragraph style by example:

1. Select a sample paragraph.

2. Use the Character and Paragraph palettes and any other commands to format the text.

3. Leave the insertion point in the formatted paragraph.

4. Choose **Type** > **Paragraph Styles**.

5. With the insertion point blinking in the formatted text, click the New Style icon. This adds a new style to the Paragraph Styles palette.

The next style allows you to automatically switch to a new style as you type text.

To set the next style:

◆ Use the Next Style pop-up list in the New Paragraph Style dialog box to choose what style is applied to the next paragraph when you press the Return key.

TIP The Next Style attribute is only available for Paragraph Styles.

Rather than create a new style from scratch, it may be easier to duplicate an existing style and then redefine it.

To duplicate a style:

1. Select the style.

2. Drag the style onto the New Style icon in the Paragraph or Character Styles palette. *(See the next page for working with character styles.)*

   or

   Choose Duplicate Style from the Paragraph or Character Styles palette submenu.

How Many Styles Do You Need?

Most of my page-layout students want to know how many styles a document needs. It depends on how many different types of paragraph elements you have.

This chapter contains 30 different paragraph and character styles. For instance, there are two types of subhead styles; one for the regular subheads and another for the ones with extra space above. There are three character styles for the body text: one for the regular text, another for the italic elements, and another for the bold elements. There is even a separate style for the single line with the word *or*.

My background using styles comes from textbook publishing where every element must conform to a style. The production people insist that designers must not use the Character or Paragraph palettes to apply any local formatting. This is so all changes to text can be applied by redefining the styles; not by highlighting text within a paragraph.

However, that is a rather rigid approach, and can cause some books to have hundreds of styles. You can use a combination of styles and local formatting.

Defining Styles

Character styles allow you to set specific attributes that override the paragraph style character attributes. For instance, the bold text within the captions of this book overrides the normal text of the captions.

To define a character style:

1. Choose **Type** > **Character Styles**. This opens the Character Styles palette 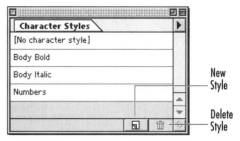.

2. Choose New Style from the Character Styles palette submenu. This opens the New Character Style dialog box ⓲.

3. Name the style.

4. Set the General controls as described on page 171.

5. Set each of the character attributes listed in the pop-up list ⓳.

6. Click OK to define the style. The name of the style appears in the Character Styles palette.

You can also define character styles by example.

To define a character style by example:

1. Select a sample paragraph.

2. Use the Character palette and other commands to format the text.

TIP It does not matter what paragraph attributes are applied to this text.

3. Leave the insertion point in the newly formatted text.

4. Choose **Type** > **Character Styles**.

5. Click the New Style icon. This adds a new style to the Character Styles palette.

New Style

Delete Style

⓱ The **Character Styles** palette.

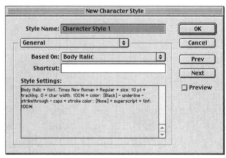

⓲ The **New Character Style** dialog box is where you can name and define character styles. The Style Settings field displays the current attributes for the style.

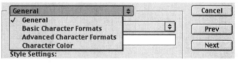

⓳ The **character attributes** in the styles pop-up list is where you can set the attributes for a character style.

Defining Styles

Style Settings:

body text + next: [Same Style] + left indent: 3p0 + first indent: -3p0

20 When you base a new style on an existing style, you can read how they differ in the Style Settings field of the New Style dialog box.

Basing one style on another allows you to quickly make variations of fundamental style. For instance, the style for the numbers in this book is based on the same style as the subheads.

To base one style on another:

1. Start with at least one paragraph or character style.

2. Open the dialog box to define a new style.

3. From the Based On pop-up menu, choose the style you wan to use as the foundation of the new style.

4. Make changes to define the second style attributes.

TIP The changes to the second style are displayed in the Style Settings area **20**.

TIP Any changes you later make to the original style also affect the second style.

You can also set keyboard shortcuts for paragraph and character styles. This makes it easy to apply styles as you type.

To set style keyboard shortcuts:

1. Open the New Paragraph Style or New Character Style dialog box.

2. Click the Shortcut field.

3. Choose a style.

4. Type the keyboard shortcut for the style.

   - The keyboard shortcut uses any combination of the modifier keys and a number from the number pad.

   - Macintosh keyboard shortcuts can use Command, Option, or Shift modifiers.

   - Windows keyboard shortcuts can use Ctrl, Alt, or Shift modifiers.

TIP In Windows, the Num Lock must be turned on to set keyboard shortcuts.

Defining Styles

Working with Styles

Defining styles is just half of the process. You take advantage of your planning when you apply the styles to text.

You can apply styles as you type new text or you can add styles to existing text.

To apply paragraph styles:

1. Select the paragraphs.

TIP You do not need to select entire paragraphs. As long as a portion is selected, the paragraph style will be applied to the entire paragraph.

2. Click the name of the paragraph style.

   or

   Type the keyboard shortcut.

When you apply a paragraph style to text, the character attributes are controlled by the Default Paragraph Style. You can replace the Default Paragraph Style by applying a character style.

To apply character styles:

1. Select the text.

TIP You must select all the text you want to format with a character style.

2. Click the name of the character style.

   or

   Type the keyboard shortcut.

Style Guidelines

Name your styles as a unit. I have four different paragraph styles for the numbered lists in this book. Each style starts with the name *list item* and is followed by a descriptive word such as *list item body, list item bullet,* and so on. This helps me recognize that the styles are applied to similar elements.

If you use keyboard shortcuts, keep them in groups. For instance, the four styles for the list items all use the keypad number 2 with variations of the keyboard modifiers. So *list item plain* is Shift-2, while *list item body* is Shift-Opt/Alt-2.

Limit how many levels you go when you base one style on another. Theoretically you can base one style on another, which is based on another, which is based on another, and so on. However, this can be confusing if you go too many levels down. I always use one style as the main one and base others on it. I think of the main style as the hub of a wheel and the others, the spokes around it.

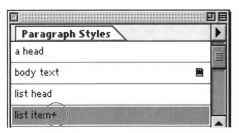

㉑ The **plus sign** next to the style name indicates that local formatting has been applied to the text.

You have a choice as to whether or not applying a style overrides any local formatting, such as bold or italic, already applied to the text.

TIP A plus sign (+) next to the paragraph style name **㉑** indicates that local formatting has been applied to the text.

To preserve local formatting:

◆ Hold the Option/Alt + Shift keys as you click the name of the paragraph style.

To override local formatting:

◆ Hold the Option/Alt keys as you click the name of the paragraph style.

TIP Styles do not override the following attributes: superscript, subscript, strikethrough, underline, language, text composer, baseline shift, and special characters.

Working with Styles

One of the advantages of using paragraph or character styles is that when you redefine the style, it changes all the existing text that has that style applied to it.

To redefine a style:

1. Select the style.

2. Double-click the style.

   or

   Choose Redefine Style from the Styles palette submenu.

   This opens the Modify Style Options dialog box, where you can change the attributes of the style.

3. Click OK. The style is redefined, and the text updates to reflect the new definition of the style.

You may have styles that you do not need in your InDesign document. You can shorten the styles list by deleting unused styles.

To delete styles:

1. Select the styles.

2. Drag the styles onto the Delete Style icon.

   or

   Choose Delete Styles from the palette submenu.

TIP If you delete a style that was applied to text, the appearance of the text does not change. The No Paragraph Style or No Character Style is applied to the text but the text is no longer associated with any style **22**.

TIP Use Select All Unused Styles to delete all the unused styles from a document.

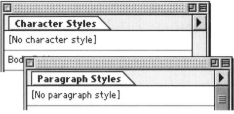

22 The No paragraph style or No character style indicates that the text is not governed by a paragraph or character style.

❷❸ The **disk icon** indicates that the style definition came from an imported text file.

You can also import or *load* styles from one InDesign document into another.

To load styles from another document:

1. Choose Load Character Styles or Load Paragraph Styles from the Styles palette submenu.

   or

   Choose Load All Styles.

2. Navigate to find the document that contains the styles you want to import.

3. Click Open. The styles are automatically added to the current document.

TIP Style names are case sensitive. A style name of *Body Text* will be added to a document that already has a style named *body text*.

TIP If you import text from a word processing program that contains styles, those styles are added to the Styles palette. A disk icon indicates that the style definition came from the imported text ❷❸.

Working with Styles

Creating Tagged Text

InDesign not only imports styles, it also allows reads formatting tags. This means you can apply codes that indicate where the formatting should be. This is very helpful if the application you are using does not support styles. For instance, you can add style tags to the text in a database ㉔ so that the text imports into InDesign correctly formatted ㉕.

You can learn the correct tags for different formatting by exporting tags from InDesign.

To export tags from InDesign:

1. Select the text you want to export.

2. Choose **File** > **Export**.

3. Choose InDesign Tagged Text from the Save As pop-up list.

4. Click Save. The Export dialog box appears ㉖.

5. Choose the type of tag:

   • Verbose shows the longer version of the tags.

   • Abbreviated shows the short version of the tags.

6. Choose the type of encoding:

   • ASCII, for most English language files.

   • ANSI, for most international characters.

   • Unicode, a standard for most languages.

   • Big 5, for Chinese characters.

   • Shift-JIS, for Japanese characters.

```
<dps:Normal=<Nextstyle:Normal><ct:>>
<ctable:=<Black:COLOR:CMYK:Process:0.0000
00,0.000000,0.000000,1.000000>>
<pstyle:Normal>The <ct:Bold>Scarecrow<ct:>
did not mind how long it took him to fill the
basket, for it enabled him to <ct:Italic>keep
away from the fire.<ct:> So he kept a good
distance away from the flames.
```

㉔ The tagged text codes as they appear outside InDesign.

The **Scarecrow** did not mind how long it took him to fill the basket, for it enabled him to *keep away from the fire.* So he kept a good distance away from the flames.

㉕ The same text as it appears on the InDesign page.

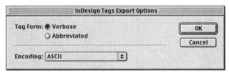

㉖ The Export Options dialog box for setting the Tagged Text options.

28 The Tags Import Options.

You can import tagged text as ordinary text. However, there are some special import options for tagged text.

To import tagged text:

1. Choose **File > Place**.

2. Navigate to find the text-only file with the tagged text codes.

3. If you want to control how the text is placed, click Show Import Options.

4. Click Open.

The tagged text import options control how any conflicts and missing tags are treated **28**.

To set tagged-text import options:

1. Select a choice for resolving conflicts between the styles in the Import Options dialog box:

   • Select Publication Definition to use the style as it is already defined in the document.

   • Select Tagged File Definition to use the style as defined in the tagged text. This adds a new style to the document with the word copy added to the style name.

2. Check Show List of Problem Tags to display a list of incorrect or unrecognized tags.

ADVANCED TEXT

The one thing that truly separates the amateurs from the experts in page layout is the control they take over the look of text. The amateurs are pleased if they can apply simple styles such as fonts, sizes, kerning, tracking, and so on.

The experts, though, want more from a page-layout program. They want sophisticated control over the kerning. This includes moving one character in so that it tucks under the stroke of another.

They want to control how lines are justified within a text frame. This means that if one line is too tightly spaced and the next is too loose, the program reapportions the space between the two lines.

They also want to add sophisticated text effects, such as automatic rules after the paragraphs. And they want total control over how text wraps around images.

These are advanced text effects. Once you apply these features to your documents, you move from the ordinary designer to the typographer.

Hanging Punctuation

One of the most sophisticated effects for text in InDesign is the ability to apply hanging punctuation to justified text. Hanging punctuation is applied by setting the *optical margin adjustment*. This moves punctuation characters slightly outside the text margin. This creates the illusion of a more uniform edge for the text ❶. In addition, optical margin adjustment also moves portions of serifs outside the margin ❷.

Optical margin adjustment is set using the Story palette.

To set optical margin adjustment:

1. Select the text.

2. Choose **Type > Story**. This opens the Story palette ❸.

3. Check Optical Margin Adjustment. The text reflows so that the punctuation and serifs lie outside the margin edges.

4. Enter a size for the amount of overhang.

TIP As a general rule, set the overhang the same size as the text.

"From the Land of Oz," said Dorothy gravely. "And here is Toto, too. And oh, Aunt Em! I'm so glad to be at home again!

"From the Land of Oz," said Dorothy gravely. "And here is Toto, too. And oh, Aunt Em! I'm so glad to be at home again!"

❶ **Optical margin adjustment** moves punctuation outside margin edges.

The Lion shook the dust out of his mane, and the Scarecrow patted himself into his best shape, and the Woodman polished his tin

❷ Optical margin adjustment moves the serifs of the drop cap outside margin edges.

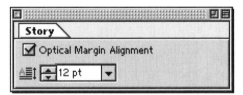

❸ The **Story palette** lets you set the optical margin adjustment to hang punctuation in the margin.

Hanging Punctuation

The road was still paved with yellow brick, but these were much covered by dried branches and dead leaves from the trees, and the walking was not at all good. — Off

The road was still paved with yellow brick, but these were much covered by dried branches and dead leaves from the trees, and the walking was not at all good. — On

❹ Turning on Multi-line Composition improves the spacing between words in this example.

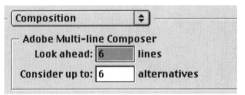

❺ The Composition Preferences allow you to control how the multiline composition occurs.

Using Multiline Composition

InDesign has two ways of compositing (laying out) text. Single-line composition looks at the current line and evaluates the best place to break the line or apply hyphenation. Multi-line composition looks at the current line as well as previous ones when it evaluates the best place to break lines. When multiline composition is turned on, the result is more even spacing for the text and fewer hyphens ❹.

To use multiline composition:

1. Select the text.

2. Choose Adobe Multi-line Composition from the Paragraph palette submenu. The text reflows.

TIP Multiline composition is a paragraph attribute and is applied to all the text in a paragraph.

TIP Multiline composition is turned on by default when you first open InDesign.

TIP Choose Adobe Single-line Composition to apply standard line-by-line composition.

You can also set how many lines InDesign looks at to determine the best line breaks.

To set the composition preferences:

1. Choose File > Preferences > Composition. The Preferences dialog box appears ❺.

2. Set the number of lines the composer analyzes before the line being edited in the Look Ahead field.

3. Set the number of alternatives that should be considered in the Consider Up To field.

TIP The higher the number you enter in these two fields, the longer it may for the lines to be composited.

TIP The composition preferences are applied to the entire document.

Applying Justification Controls

Justification determines how lines fit between margins. For instance, the lines in this paragraph come as close as possible to the end of the margin with a certain amount of space between the words. InDesign provides three different ways to control justification.

Word spacing changes the space between words. *Letter spacing* changes the space between letters. *Glyph scaling* changes the shape of the letters. *(See the sidebar on the next page for a discussion of the best settings.)*

To set word spacing:

1. Select the text.

2. Choose Justification from the Paragraph palette submenu. This opens the Justification dialog box ❻.

3. Set the Word Spacing options as follows:

   • Set the Desired field to your preferred amount of space between words. 100% indicates that you want the same amount that the designer of the typeface created.

   • Set the Minimum field to the smallest amount of space you want between words. For instance, a value of 80% means that you are willing to allow the space to be 80% of the normal space.

   • Set the Maximum field to the largest amount of space you want between words. A value of 120% means that you are willing to allow the space to be 120% of the normal space.

4. Click OK to apply the changes ❼.

TIP The Minimum, Desired, and Maximum settings apply only to text that is set to one of the Justified settings. Other alignments, such as left-aligned text, use only the Desired setting.

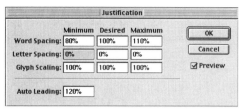

❻ The **Justification** dialog box controls the word and letter spacing.

Min: 80, Desired: 100, Max: 120

Welcome, my child, to the Land of Oz

Min: 80, Desired: 100, Max: 100

Welcome, my child, to the Land of Oz

❼ The effects of changing the word spacing.

Min: 0%, Desired: 0%, Max: 0%

Welcome, my child, to the Land of Oz

Min: -4%, Desired: 0%, Max: 4%

Welcome, my child, to the Land of Oz

❽ The effect of changing the letter spacing.

The space between letters is *letter spacing*. This is sometimes called character spacing.

To set letter spacing:

1. Select the text.

2. Choose Justification from the Paragraph palette submenu.

3. Set the Letter Spacing options as follows:

- Set the Desired field to your preferred amount of space between letters. 0% indicates that you do not want to add or subtract any space.

- Set the Minimum field to the smallest amount of space you want between words. A value of –5% allows the space to be reduced by 5% of the normal space.

- Set the Maximum field to the largest amount of space you want between words. A value of 5% allows the space to be increased by 5% of the normal space.

4. Click OK to apply the changes ❽.

TIP If a paragraph cannot be set using the justification controls you choose, InDesign violates the settings by adding or subtracting spaces. Set the Composition preferences to have those violations highlighted *(see page 242)*.

What Are the Best Justification Settings?

Perhaps the most debated issue in desktop publishing is what are the best settings for the Justification controls. The answer depends on a variety of factors. The typeface, width of the columns, even the type of text all need to be considered in setting the Justification controls.

For body text I use word spacing of 70%, 100%, and 110%. In New York, we like to set copy so it fits tightly. However, for headlines, I get even tighter with word spacing of 60%, 90%, 100%.

I keep all the letter spacing values at 0%. I set all the glyph spacing values at 100%. I don't like to scrunch up letter spacing and I definitely don't like to change the shape of the text.

But that's just me. And that's why they call them preferences!

Another way to control justification is to use *glyph scaling*. Glyph scaling applies horizontal scaling to the text so it takes up more or less space within the line.

To set glyph scaling:

1. Select the text.

2. Choose Justification from the Paragraph palette submenu.

3. Set the Glyph Scaling options as follows:

   • Set the Desired field to your preferred amount of scaling. 0% indicates that you do not want to apply any scaling to the character shape.

   • Set the Minimum field to the smallest amount of scaling that you are willing to apply to the text. A value of –5% means that you are willing to allow the characters to be reduced by 5% of their normal width.

   • Set the Maximum field to the amount that you are willing to expand the space between words. A value of 5% means that you are willing to allow the characters to be increased by 5% of their normal width.

4. Click OK to apply the changes ❾.

TIP Glyph scaling distorts the shape of letters. Typographic purists (such as this author) try to avoid distorting the letterforms whenever possible ❿.

The Auto Leading field controls how much space is set between lines when the auto leading is chosen *(see page 48)*.

To set the Auto Leading percentage:

1. Choose Justification from the Paragraph palette submenu.

2. Enter an amount in the Auto Leading field.

TIP Most professional designers use an absolute amount for leading, rather than the automatic leading.

The road was still paved with yellow brick, but these were much covered by dried branches and dead leaves from the trees, and the walking was not at all good.

Min: 100%, Desired: 100%, Max: 100%

The road was still paved with yellow brick, but these were much covered by dried branches and dead leaves from the trees, and the walking was not at all good.

Min: 80%, Desired: 100%, Max: 120%

❾ The effects of changing the **glyph scaling**.

❿ How glyph spacing distorts a letterform. The gray area shows the distorted shape. The black area shows the original shape of the character.

⓫ The Paragraph palette allows you to turn on hyphenation for selected text.

⓬ The **Hyphenation** dialog box controls how InDesign applies hyphenation.

Controlling Hyphenation

InDesign lets you turn on hyphenation in the Paragraph palette. Once hyphenation is turned on, you can then control how the hyphenation is applied. *(See the sidebar on this page for comments on setting the hyphenation controls.)*

To turn on hyphenation:

1. Select the text.

2. Check Hyphenate in the Paragraph palette **⓫**.

To control the hyphenation:

1. Select Hyphenation from the Paragraph palette submenu. The Hyphenation dialog box appears **⓬**.

2. Set the hyphenation controls as follow:

   - Set the minimum numbers of letters a word must be before it can be hyphenated in the Words Longer Than field.

   - Set the minimum number of letters that must appear before the hyphen in the After First field.

   - Set the minimum number of letters that must appear after the hyphen in the Before Last field.

   - Set how many consecutive lines that end with hyphens can appear in the Hyphen Limit field.

   - Click Hyphenate Capitalized Words to allow those words to be hyphenated.

3. Click OK to apply the controls.

Setting hyphenation controls

My own preference is to set the Words Longer Than to six or more. This allows a word such as *person* to be hyphenated.

I also prefer a minimum of three letters before the hyphen and three after. This avoids breaking words as *un-excited* or *relunctant-ly.*

Hyphenate capitalized words?

Some people automatically turn this off. I don't. The command doesn't distinguish between proper nouns and words that begin a sentence. So I would rather set the proper nouns not to break by using the No Break command *(see page 186)* or by inserting a discretionary hyphen *(see page 187)* before the word.

Controlling Hyphenation

You can also control hyphenation in Flush Left text by setting the hyphenation zone. The hyphenation zone determines how close to the end of a line the entire word must fall in order to be hyphenated ⓭.

To set the hyphenation zone:

1. Select the text.

2. Choose Hyphenation from the Paragraph palette submenu.

3. Enter the distance in the Hyphenation Zone field.

4. Click OK.

TIP The Hyphenation Zone applies only to text set with the Single-line Composer.

Sometimes you may want to prevent words or phrases from being hyphenated or breaking across lines. For instance, you might not want the words Mr. Cohen to be separated at the end of a line. You might not want a compound word such as self-effacing to be broken with another hyphen ⓮.

To apply the no break command:

1. Select the text.

2. Choose No Break from the Character palette submenu.

The Lion shook the dust out of his mane, and the Scarecrow patted himself into his best shape, and the Woodman polished his tin. When they were all quite presentable they followed the soldier into a big room.

0p zone

The Lion shook the dust out of his mane, and the Scarecrow patted himself into his best shape, and the Woodman polished his tin. When they were all quite presentable they followed the soldier into a big room.

3p zone

⓭ The effect of setting a **hyphenation zone** on text. Notice that the higher the hyphenation zone, the less likely that words will be divided.

Behold! I am the great and mighty, all-powerful Oz. There are none who can match my majestic power and glory.

Behold! I am the great and mighty, all-powerful Oz. There are none who can match my majestic power and glory.

⓮ In this example the word powerful was selected and the **No Break** command was applied to prevent the text from hyphenating.

A·document· can·not·be· considered·

⓯ A discretionary hyphen appears within the word but prints only when it at the end of a line.

You can also control hyphenation by inserting a *discretionary hyphen,* which forces the word to hyphenate at that point if it falls at the end of a line.

To use a discretionary hyphen:

1. Place the insertion point where you want the hyphen to occur.

2. Press Command/Ctrl-Shift-(hyphen).

   or

   Control/Right-click and choose **Insert Special Character > Discretionary Hyphen** from the contextual menu.

TIP The discretionary hyphen prints only when it appears at the end of the line **⓯**.

TIP Insert a discretionary hyphen before a word to prevent that instance of the word from being hyphenated.

You can also edit the dictionary to control hyphenation.

To edit the hyphenation in the dictionary:

1. Choose **Edit > Edit Dictionary**.

2. Type the word you want to edit.

3. Click Hyphenate to display the possible hyphenation points.

   - Insert one tilde (~) to indicate the best possible hyphenation position.

   - Insert two tildes (~~) to indicate the next best possible position.

   - Insert three tildes (~~~) to indicate the least acceptable position.

   - Insert a tilde before the word to prevent the word from being hyphenated.

3. Click Add to add the new hyphenation to the dictionary.

Controlling Hyphenation

Keeping Lines Together

Another technique to control text is to specify how many lines of text must remain together in a column or page. This is commonly called controlling the paragraph widows. InDesign does this using the Keep Options.

To set the keep options for a paragraph:

1. Choose Keep Options from the Paragraph palette submenu. This opens the Keep Options dialog box **⑯**.

2. Enter a number in the Keep With Next Lines field to force the last line in a paragraph to stay in the same column or page with the specified number of lines.

TIP This option ensures that subheads or titles remain in the same column as the body copy that follows.

3. Click Keep Lines Together and set the options as follows:

   • All Lines in Paragraph prevents the paragraph from ever breaking.

   • At Start/End of Paragraph lets you set the number of lines that must remain together for the start and the end of the paragraph.

3. Use the Start Paragraph pop-up list **⑰** to choose where the lines must jump to.

   • Anywhere allows the text to jump anywhere.

   • In Next Column forces the text to the next column or page.

   • On Next Page forces the text to the next page.

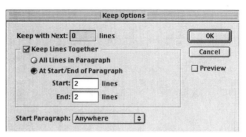

⑯ The **Keep Options** dialog box controls how the lines of paragraphs break across columns or pages.

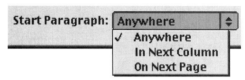

⑰ The **Start Paragraph** pop-up list lets you choose where the next lines of the paragraph appear.

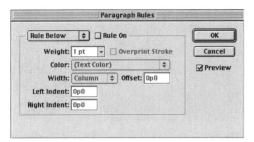

⓲ The **Paragraph Rules** dialog box controls the appearance of the paragraph rules.

Working with Paragraph Rules

If you want a paragraph to have a line (technically called a *rule*) to appear above or below a paragraph, you might be tempted to draw a line using the Pen or the Line tool. Unfortunately if the text reflows, a drawn line does not travel with the text. You could also paste the line into the text as an inline graphic *(see page 131)*, but there are limits to how much you can control those lines.

Paragraph rules allow you to create lines that travel with the paragraph and that can be applied as part of style sheets *(see page 168)*.

TIP It may seem like more work to use paragraph rules, but they save you time in the long run.

To apply paragraph rules:

1. Select the text.

2. Choose Paragraph Rules from the Paragraph palette submenu. This opens the Paragraph Rules dialog box ⓲.

3. Set the options as follows:

- Choose Rule Above or Rule Below from the pop-up list to specify whether the rule appears before or after the selected paragraph.

- Check Rule On to turn the rule on.

- Set an amount for the weight (or thickness) of the rule.

- Check Overprint Stroke to set the ink to overprint *(see page 110 for setting overprints)*.

- Use the Color pop-up list to apply a color to the rule.

TIP Rules are colored only with named colors from the Swatches palette. *(For more information on working with colors, see Chapter 6, "Working in Color.")*

True Story

When I first started learning page layout software, I used the art director's computer at the advertising agency where I worked. I stayed after hours to explore the programs and create documents.

When I saw the command Rules in the menu, I figured that was where they kept the laws governing the program. Since I didn't want to mess up the art director's machine, I never chose the command.

It was several years later (and several horrible jobs without paragraph rules) that I found out what the Rules were.

The size of a rule depends on several factors. The rule can be set to cover the width of the column or the width of the text. The rule can also be set to be indented from the column or text margins.

To control the length of a rule:

1. Choose Column or Text from the width pop-up list in the Paragraph Rules dialog box.

   Column rules are the width of the column. Text rules are the width of the closest line of text ⓮.

2. Set the Left Indent to the amount that the rule should be indented from the left side of the column or text.

3. Set the Right Indent to the amount that the rule should be indented from the right side of the column or text.

TIP Use positive numbers to move the rule in from the margin. Use negative numbers to move the rule outside the margin. The rule can extend outside the text frame ⓴.

By default the paragraph rule is positioned on the baseline of the text. You can control the position above or below the baseline ㉑. This is called the *offset* of the rule.

To control the offset of a rule:

2. In the Paragraph Rules dialog box, enter a value in the Offset field.

- For a Rule Above, positive numbers raise the rule above the baseline.

- For a Rule Below, positive numbers lower the rule below the baseline.

TIP Negative numbers move rules in the opposite direction.

"From the Land of Oz," said Dorothy gravely. "And here is Toto, too. And oh, Aunt Em! I'm so glad to be at home again! — Column

"From the Land of Oz," said Dorothy gravely. "And here is Toto, too. And oh, Aunt Em! I'm so glad to be at home again! — Text

⓮ **Column rules** fit to the width of the column. **Text rules** fit to the neighboring text.

"From the Land of Oz," said Dorothy gravely. "And here is Toto, too. And oh, Aunt Em! I'm so glad to be at home again! — No Indent

"From the Land of Oz," said Dorothy gravely. "And here is Toto, too. And oh, Aunt Em! I'm so glad to be at home again! — Indents Applied

⓴ How changing the **Left and Right Indent** settings changes the look of rules.

"From the Land of Oz," said Dorothy gravely. "And here is Toto, too. And oh, Aunt Em! I'm so glad to be at home again! — 0 pt. Offset

"From the Land of Oz," said Dorothy gravely. "And here is Toto, too. And oh, Aunt Em! I'm so glad to be at home again! — 10 pt. Offset

㉑ How changing the **Offset** affects the position of rules. Here a rule below the paragraph has an offset of 10 points.

Working with Paragraph Rules

Chapter Ten: The Guardian of the Gate

It was some time before the Cowardly Lion awakened, for he had lain among the poppies a long while,

㉒ A paragraph rule can create the effect of reversed text.

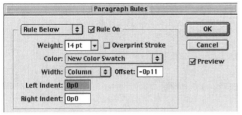

㉓ A sample dialog box to create the effect of reversed text using a paragraph rule.

You can create many special effects with paragraph rules. One of the most common is to superimpose text inside paragraph rules to create the effect of reversed text. Most reversed text is white type inside a black background. However, any light color can be used inside any dark background **㉒**.

To reverse text using rules:

1. Apply a light color to a line of type.

2. Open the Paragraph Rules dialog box.

3. Create a Rule Below.

4. Set the weight of the rule to a point size large enough to enclose the text. For instance, if the text is 12 points, the rule should be at least 12 points.

TIP If you have more than one line of text, you need to calculate the size of the leading times the number of lines.

5. Set a negative number for the offset value.

TIP The offset amount should be slightly less than the weight of the rule. For instance a rule of 14 points might take an offset of −11 points.

6. Check Preview so you can see the effect of the weight and offset settings you choose **㉓**.

7. Adjust the weight and offset, if necessary.

8. Click OK to apply the rule.

Working with Paragraph Rules

Wrapping Text

You can also control how text flows around images and other objects. This is called the *text wrap*.

To apply a text wrap:

1. Select the object that you want the text to run around. This can be an imported graphic, a text frame, or an unassigned frame.

2. Choose **Object > Text Wrap**. This opens the Text Wrap palette **24**.

3. Choose one of the following options **25** for how the text should flow around the object.

   - Bounding Box flows the text around the bounding box for the object.

   - Object Shape flows the text around the shape of the frame.

   - Jump Object flows the text to the next available space under the object.

   - Jump to Next Column flows the text to the next column or text frame.

4. Check Invert to force the text to flow inside the offset path **26**.

5. Set the distance that the text should stay away from the object in the offset fields **27**.

TIP The number of available offset fields changes depending on the type of text wrap you choose.

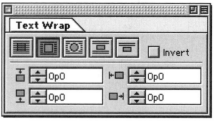

24 The **Text Wrap** palette controls how text flows around an object.

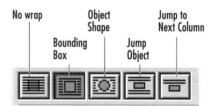

25 The five text wrap controls.

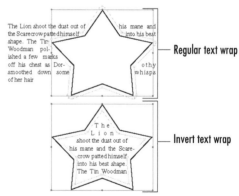

26 The Invert command forces text to flow inside the area of the text wrap.

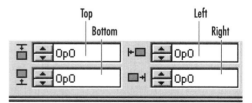

27 The offset fields allow you to set how far the text stays away from an object that it wraps around or within.

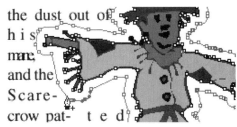

28 Position the Pen tool over a path and click to add points to a text wrap path.

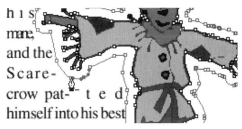

29 Position the Pen tool over a point and click to delete points from a text wrap path.

30 Use the Direct Selection tool to change the shape of a text wrap path.

Once you set a text wrap, you can still manipulate it so that the text wraps more legibly or fits more attractively into the contour of the object. This is called a *custom text wrap*.

To create a custom text wrap:

1. Select the object that has the text wrap applied to it.

2. Click the Pen tool on an empty space on the text wrap path to add a new point to the path 28.

3. Click the Pen tool on a point on the text wrap path to delete the point from the path 29.

4. Use the Direct Selection tool to manipulate the points on the text wrap path 30.

TIP Hold the Command/Ctrl key to access the Direction Selection tool while in the Pen tool.

Wrapping Text

COLOR MANAGEMENT

I remember when my family bought our first color television set. Back in those days there weren't many programs broadcast in color. So color was a strange and mysterious thing. No one in the family understood how it worked. We didn't know how to make the pictures look realistic. We jumped up to change the image whenever we changed channels. Basically we spent most of our time fiddling with the TV controls rather than just watching the shows. Or if we couldn't get acceptable color, we watched black and white programs.

Well, that's a lot like managing color today in desktop publishing. Not many people understand how to manage it. They don't know what the best look should be. They don't know how to control images from different applications. Basically they spend most of their time fiddling with the controls. Or, if they can't deal with color management, they do nothing.

The truth is that color is an extremely deep and complex subject—far too deep for the scope of this book. In this chapter I give you some basic steps to use InDesign to manage color.

Choosing Application Color Settings

The first step for color management is to set the application color settings. These are the settings that control all InDesign documents.

The color engine is the system used to control the color management. Various companies make their own color engines. Adobe makes its own color engine, which ships with InDesign.

To choose the color engine:

1. Choose **File** >**Color Settings** > **Application Color Settings.** This opens the Application Color Settings dialog box ❶.

2. Use the Engine pop-up list to choose a color-management engine:

   • Choose Adobe CMS engine if you are working with other Adobe products.

   • Choose another engine, such as Kodak or Lino, depending on what your print shop recommends.

TIP Your service bureau or print shop may provide you with a custom setting file for the color engine they use. You can install it so that it appears on this list.

2. Click OK to save the settings.

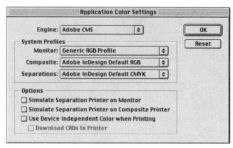

❶ The **Application Color Settings** dialog box controls the color settings for all InDesign documents.

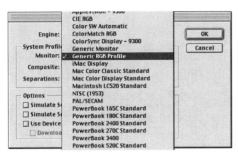

❷ The **Monitor profiles** allow you to choose the type of monitor you use to view your documents.

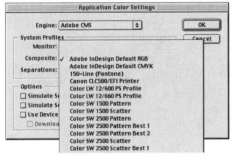

❸ The **Composite profile list** allows you to choose the type of printer you use for proofing color documents.

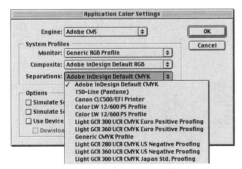

❹ The **Separations profile list** allows you to choose the type of final output device your color work will be printed on.

In addition to the color-management engine, you need to choose a system profile.

To set the system profile:

1. Choose File > Color Settings > Application Color Settings.

2. Choose a monitor profile that most closely matches your own computer screen from the Monitor pop-up list ❷.

   If you do not see your monitor, choose Generic RGB Profile.

   TIP If you have previously calibrated your monitor and saved a custom profile setting, it appears in this list.

3. Choose a composite profile that best fits the printer you use for color proofing from the Composite pop-up list ❸. This could be a color ink-jet printer or a laser printer.

   If you do not have a composite device, choose Adobe InDesign Default RGB.

   TIP Select Simulate Separation Printer on Composite to send the separations information to the composite printer.

4. Choose a separation profile that best fits your CMYK output from the Separations pop-up list ❹.

   If you do not know the type of separation profile, choose Adobe InDesign Default CMYK.

   TIP Select Simulate Separation Printer on Monitor to send the separations information to the monitor.

   TIP If your printer supports PostScript device-independent color, choose Use Device Independent Color When Printing.

Choosing Application Color Settings

Choosing Document Color Settings

In addition to the application settings, you need to set the color-management options for each document.

To set the source profiles:

1. Choose File > Color Settings > Document Color Settings. This opens the Document Color Settings dialog box ❺.

2. Check Enable Color Management to turn on color management.

3. For CMYK colors, choose a source profile from the CMYK pop-up list ❻.

   Adobe recommends Use Separations Profile to match the separations profile set in the application settings. Use another setting if the document is to be printed on a different printer.

4. For LAB colors, choose a profile from the LAB pop-up list ❼.

   To have InDesign control LAB colors, choose Adobe InDesign Default LAB.

5. For RGB colors, choose a profile from the RGB pop-up list ❽.

   To have InDesign control RGB colors, choose Adobe InDesign Default RGB.

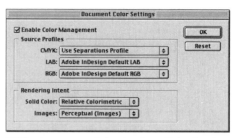

❺ The **Document Color Settings** dialog box lets you turn on color management.

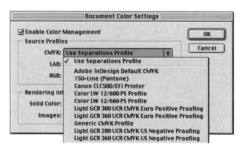

❻ The **CMYK profiles** can be used to set specific separations for each document.

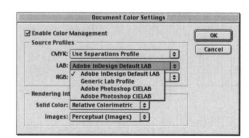

❼ The **LAB profiles** can be used to set the profiles for LAB colors.

❽ The **RGB profiles** can be used to set the profiles for RGB colors.

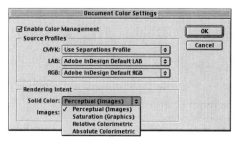

⑨ The Renedering Color Settings dialog box set for **solid colors.**

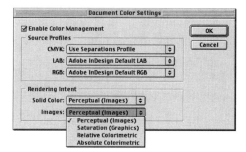

⑩ The Renedering Color Settings dialog box set for **photograph images.**

You can also set the rendering intent for the current document to specify how to display colors in graphics created in InDesign and imported from other programs.

To set the rendering intent:

1. Choose **File > Color Settings > Document Color Settings.**

2. Click Enable Color Management to turn on color management.

3. For nonphotographic images, select a choice from the Solid Color pop-up list **⑨**.

TIP Adobe recommends Relative Colorimetric as the best choice for flat colors.

4. For photographic image, select a choice from the Images pop-up list **⑩**.

TIP Adobe recommends Perceptual (Images) as the best choice for photographic images.

Choosing Document Color Settings

Controlling Imported Graphics

You can also set color management for imported images.

To set the color management for imported images:

1. Choose Show Import Options in the Place dialog box. This opens the Image Import Options dialog box. *(For more information on placing images, see Chapter 7, "Imported Graphics.")*

2. Choose Color Settings from the pop-up list. This displays the color management settings ⓫.

3. Choose Enable Color Management to turn on color management for that file.

4. Choose the profile from the pop-up list.

   Choose Use Document Default to have the document settings applied to the graphic.

5. Choose a rendering intent from the pop-up list.

TIP Adobe recommends Perceptual (Images) for photographic images.

Once you have imported a graphic, you can change the color-management settings without having to reimport the graphic.

To change color management for placed images:

1. Select the graphic.

2. Choose **Object >Image Color Settings.** This opens the Image Color Settings dialog box for that image.

3. Set the profile and rendering as described on the previous pages of this section.

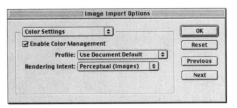

⓫ The **Color settings** for the Image Import Options.

OUTPUT 12

Several years ago the title of this chapter would have been *Printing*. That was what you did with page-layout documents. You printed them using a desktop printer. Today, however, there are far more choices for your InDesign documents.

These days, the term printing is too limited. Printing is what you do when you send a document to a desktop printer. InDesign files are created as part of the professional prepress process. (For more information on professional printing see *The Non-Designer's Scan and Print Book* by Sandee Cohen and Robin Williams.) So you need to know more than just how to print to a desktop printer. You need to know how to make sure your document has been setup correctly. You need to know what files are necessary to send to a print shop.

So this chapter is called Output. Output refers to preparing files and printing them—to either an ordinary desktop printer or with a service-bureau imagesetter.

Printing a Document

When a document is printed, there are many different instructions that are sent to the printer. You need to set all those instructions correctly.

To print a document:

1. Choose **File**>**Print.** This opens the Print dialog box for either Windows ❶ or Mac ❷.

2. If necessary, set the following options:

   • Choose a printer as described on the following page.

   • Set the paper properties as described on page 204.

   • Set the graphics properties (Win) as described on page 205.

   • Set the PostScript and layout options (Mac) as described on page 206.

   • Set the page controls as described on page 207.

   • Set the color controls as described on page 208.

   • Set the page resizing controls as described on page 209.

   • Set the tiling as described on page 210.

   • Add any page marks as described on page 211.

   TIP You do not need to set all the controls every time you print unless you need to change a specific setting.

3. Click OK (Win) or Print (Mac) to print the document.

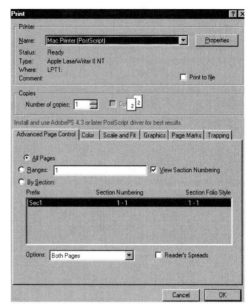

❶ The Windows **Print dialog box** controls the printing instructions.

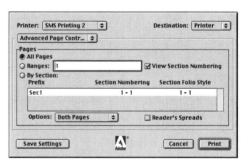

❷ The Macintosh **Print dialog box** controls the printing instructions.

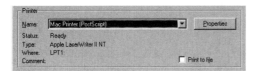

❸ The Windows **Name list** lets you choose the printer to print a document.

❹ The Macintosh **Printer list** lets you choose the printer to print a document.

Choosing a Printer

Before you print, you need to choose which printer will print your file.

To choose the printer (Win):

1. Choose **File** > **Print.** This opens the Print dialog box.

2. Choose the printer from the Name list at the top of the dialog box ❸.

To choose the printer (Mac):

1. Choose **File** > **Page Setup.** This opens the Page Setup dialog box.

2. Choose a printer from the Printer list at the top of the dialog box ❹.

TIP You can also select the printer by choosing **File** > **Print.** However, the Page Setup dialog box gives you easy access to the paper properties settings, as shown in the next exercise.

Choosing a Printer

Setting the Paper Properties

The paper properties let you set the size of the paper as well as the orientation of the document on the printed page.

To set the paper properties (Win):

1. Click Properties in the Print dialog box to open the Printer Properties.

2. Click the Paper tab. This displays the paper properties ➎. Choose the page size from the choices in the window.

3. Choose the Orientation:

   • Portrait sets the document so that the width is shorter than the height.

   • Landscape sets the document so that the height is shorter than the width.

   • If you choose Landscape, you can check Rotated, to rotate the image 180 degrees.

4. Use the Paper Source pop-up list to choose a cassette or manual feed.

To set the paper properties (Mac):

1. Choose **File** > **Page Setup.** This opens the Page Setup dialog box.

2. Choose Page Attributes from the pop-up list. Choose the page size from the Paper pop-up list ➏.

3. Choose the Orientation:

   • Portrait sets the document so that the width is shorter than the height.

   • Landscape sets the document so that the height is shorter than the width.

To set the paper source (Mac):

1. Choose **File** > **Print.**

2. Choose General from the pop-up list

3. Use the Paper Source pop-up list to choose Cassette or Manual Feed ➐.

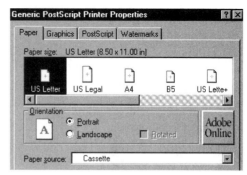

➎ The **Paper Properties** (Win) lets you set the page size, orientation, and paper casette.

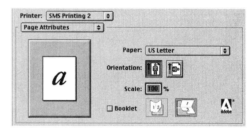

➏ The **Page Attributes** (Mac) lets you set the page size and the orientation.

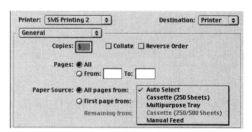

➐ The **General settings** (Mac) of the Print dialog box let you choose the cassette tray for printing.

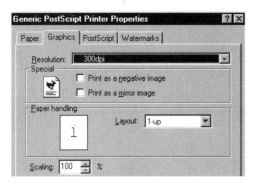

 The **Graphics properties** (**Win**) let you control the look and layout of the printed document.

Setting Graphics Properties (Win)

The Graphics properties let you set how the pages are to be printed. Some of these options are used only when printing to an imagesetter. Others can help you print more than one page on a piece of paper.

To set the graphics properties (Win):

1. Click Properties in the Print dialog box.

2. Click the Graphics tab. This opens the Graphics options ❽.

3. If the printer has different resolution settings, choose a resolution.

4. Check Print as a Negative Image to change the black areas to white and the white areas to black.

5. Check Print as a Mirror Image to reverse the document.

TIP The negative and mirror-image settings are usually reserved for outputting to film.

6. Use the settings in the Layout pop-up list to print more than one page on each piece of paper.

7. Set an amount in the Scaling field to reduce or enlarge the page.

Setting Graphics Properties (Win)

Setting PostScript and Layout Options (Mac)

The PostScript and Layout options let you set how the pages are to be printed.

To set the PostScript options (Mac):

1. Choose **File** > **Page Setup**.

2. Choose PostScript Options from the pop-up list. This opens the PostScript options **9**.

3. Check the Visual Effects as follows:

- Flip Horizontal creates a mirror image of the document from left to right.

- Flip Vertical creates a mirror image of the document from top to bottom.

- Invert Image changes black areas to white, and white areas to black.

TIP The Visual Effects commands are usually reserved for outputting to film.

To set the Layout options (Mac):

1. Choose **File** > **Print**.

2. Choose Layout from the pop-up list. This opens the Layout options **10**.

3. Use the Pages Per Sheet (pgs/sheet) settings in the pop-up list to print more than one page on each piece of paper.

   or

   Use the Sheets Per Page (sheets/pg) settings to increase the size of the document page so that only a portion prints on each piece of paper **11**.

4. If you print more than one page on a piece of paper, click the Layout Direction icons to set the printing order for the pages.

5. If you print more than one page on a piece of paper, use the Border pop-up list to add a border that is printed between pages.

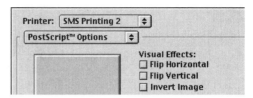

9 The **PostScript Options** (Mac) let you control how the document prints.

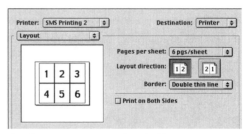

10 The **Layout Options** (Mac) allow you to control how the document pages are printed on each piece of paper.

11 The **Pages Per Sheet** (Mac) let you enlarge one page so that it prints on multiple sheets of paper.

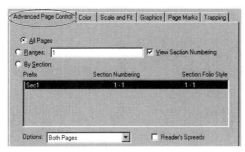

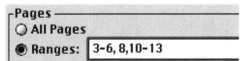 Click the tab to display the **Advanced Page Controls (Win)**.

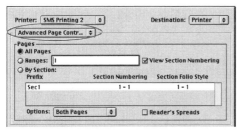

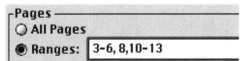 Use the pop-up list to display the **Advanced Page Controls (Mac)**.

Pages
○ All Pages
● Ranges: 3-6, 8,10-13

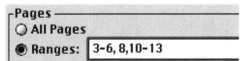 You can use a combination of page ranges and individual pages when exporting PDF files. Here pages 3 through 6, 8, and 10 through 13 are set to be printed.

Setting the Advanced Page Controls

InDesign gives you advanced controls for choosing which pages should be printed.

To set the pages to be printed:

1. Choose **File > Print**.

2. Click the Advanced Page Controls tab (Win) 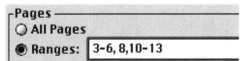 or choose Advanced Page Controls from the pop-up list (Mac) 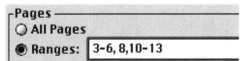. This opens the Advanced Page Controls section of the Print dialog box.

3. Choose the pages to print as follows:

   - All Pages outputs all the pages in the document.

   - By Section exports specific sections of a document. *(For more information on creating sections, see Chapter 8, "Long Documents.")*

   - Ranges let you specify certain pages. Use a hyphen to specify a range of pages, such as 4–6. Use a comma to specify individual pages, such as 8, 9.

   TIP You can combine ranges and individual pages in one field 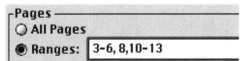.

4. Set the Options as follows:

   - Both Pages prints the even- and odd-numbered pages.

   - Even Pages Only prints only even-numbered pages.

   - Odd Pages Only prints only odd-numbered pages.

   TIP Use the even or odd options to print odd pages on one side of the paper, and then put the paper back in the printer to print even pages on the other side of the paper.

5. Click Reader's Spreads to print pages as they would be bound in a publication.

Setting the Advanced Page Controls

Setting Color Controls

You may need to set the color controls to choose how color documents are printed.

To set the color controls:

1. Choose **File** > **Print**.

2. Click the Color tab (Win) ⓯ or choose Color from the pop-up list (Mac) ⓰. This opens the Color section of the Print dialog box.

3. Choose Composite to print all the colors onto one page.

   or

   Choose Separations to print each color on its own plate.

   TIP Separations printed on a laser printer are commonly called *paper separations* and are used to make sure the proper number of plates will be printed by service bureau.

4. If you choose Separations, you can set use the Screening list to set the frequency and angle for the halftone screens.

   TIP You can also use the frequency and angle fields to set your own settings.

5. If you choose Separations, you can choose each color and uncheck Print This Ink to prevent the color from being printed ⓱.

   TIP Use the Print All Inks and Print No Inks buttons to quickly turn on and off the settings for all the colors.

6. If you have any spot colors in the document that you want to print as process color, click All to Process to convert them to process colors.

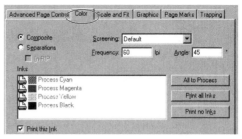

⓯ Click the tab for the **Color section** (Win).

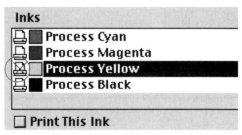

⓰ Use the pop-up list to display the **Color section** (Mac).

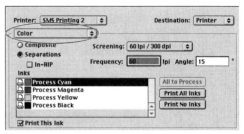

⓱ Uncheck **Print This Ink** to prevent a color from being printed.

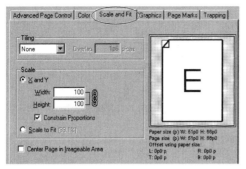

⑱ Click the tab to display the **Scale and Fit** controls (Win).

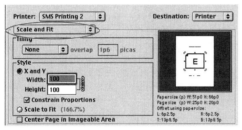

⑲ Use the pop-up list to display the **Scale and Fit** controls (Mac).

Resizing to Fit Paper Sizes

You may want to scale a page to fit a certain printer paper size. Rather than change the actual size of the document, you can use the Scale and Fit options.

To set the Scale and Fit options:

1. Choose **File** > **Print**.

2. Click the Scale and Fit tab (Win) **⑱** or choose Scale and Fit from the pop-up list (Mac) **⑲**. This opens the Scale and Fit section of the Print dialog box.

3. Use the Scale controls to reduce or enlarge the page when printed.

4. Check Scale to Fit to automatically reduce or enlarge the page to fit the paper chosen in the Paper Properties dialog box *(see page 204)*.

5. Check Center Page in Imageable Area to print the document page in the center of the paper.

TIP The preview area changes as you choose each of the settings.

Resizing to Fit Paper Sizes

Tiling Pages

If your document is larger that the paper, you can print portions on several different pages. You can then assemble those pages together. This is called *tiling*.

To set automatic tiling:

1. Choose **File > Print.**

2. Click the Scale and Fit tab (Win) or choose Scale and Fit from the pop-up list (Mac).

3. Choose Auto from the Tiling pop-up list.

4. Set the amount in the Overlap field. This controls how much of one page is duplicated on the tile for a second section of the page.

You can also tile pages manually. This lets you make sure that the edge of the paper does not cut across an important portion of the page.

To set manual tiling:

1. Use the zero-point crosshairs on the ruler to set the upper-left corner of the area you want to print ❷⓿. *(For more information on setting the zero point of the ruler, see Chapter 2, "Document Setup.")*

2. Choose **File > Print.**

3. Click the Scale and Fit tab (Win) or choose Scale and Fit from the pop-up list (Mac).

4. Choose Manual from the Tiling pop-up list.

5. Click Print to print that one page.

6. Reposition the zero-point crosshairs to set a new area to be printed.

7. Follow steps 2 through 5 to define and print the second tile.

8. Repeat the process until the entire page has been printed.

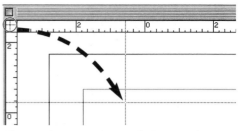

❷⓿ Move the zero-point crosshairs to set the area to print as a tile on one page.

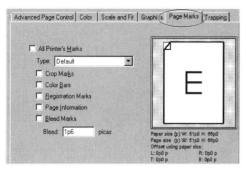

㉑ Click the tab to display the **Page Marks** controls (Win).

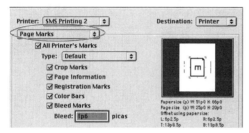

㉒ Use the pop-up list to display the **Page Marks** controls (Mac).

Bleed marks

Tint bars   Color bars

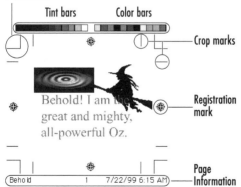

Crop marks

Registration mark

Page Information

㉓ The **Page Marks** as they appear on the printed page.

Adding Page Marks

You can also add information that shows where the document should be trimmed, the name of the document, and so on. This information is sometimes called *printer's marks* or *page marks*.

To set the page marks:

1. Choose **File** > **Print**.

2. Click the Page Marks tab (Win) **㉑** or choose Page Marks from the pop-up list (Mac) **㉒**. This opens the Page Marks section of the Print dialog box.

3. Check All Printer's Marks to turn on all the marks or use the checkboxes to set each one individually **㉓**:

   • Crop Marks indicates where the page should be trimmed.

   • Page Information prints the name of the file, page number, and time the document was printed.

   • Registration Marks adds small crosshair targets that are used to line up pieces of film.

   • Color Bars provides boxes that display the colors used in the document as well as the tint bars that can be used to calibrate the printing press for correct tints of colors.

   • Bleed Marks show how far outside the crop marks you must put graphics so that they are trimmed correctly.

   • If you set Bleed Marks, you can set the amount in the Bleed field to choose how far away from the crop marks the bleed marks are positioned.

TIP Your service bureau or print shop can give you the correct size for bleed marks.

TIP The preview area of the Print dialog box shows the marks around the page.

Creating a Preflight Report

When you create an InDesign document, you have two jobs, designer and production manager. As the designer you can easily see your errors. But as the production manager, you may not realize that the color you have created will not print correctly or that the image you placed is the wrong resolution or format. Fortunately, InDesign has a built-in preflight utility that checks all the elements in your document to make sure they print correctly. (The name comes from the list that airline pilots must complete before they take off.)

To run the preflight utility:

1. Choose **File** > **Preflight**. InDesign takes a moment to check all the elements of the document and then opens the Preflight dialog box.

2. Review the information in the Preflight Summary **㉔**.

TIP The Package command is available in the Preflight dialog box. This is the same as the Package command located on the File menu. *(See page 215 for more information on the Package command.)*

To review the Fonts information:

◆ Choose Fonts from the pop-up list at the top of the Preflight dialog box. This opens the fonts information **㉕**, which shows the type of font as whether it is installed in the system.

TIP Your Service Bureau may ask you to use only Type 1 fonts. The Fonts information dialog box lets you check to make sure you are using the correct fonts.

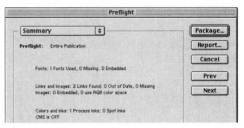

㉔ The **Preflight Summary** contains an overview of all the information assembled by the Preflight utility.

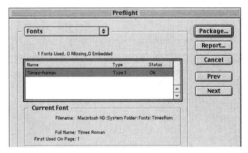

㉕ The **Fonts information** lets you check the status of the fonts.

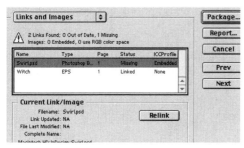

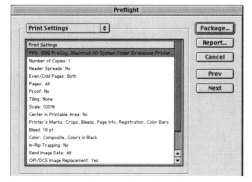

26 The **Links information** lets you check the status of placed graphics.

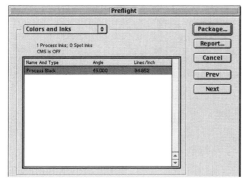

27 The **Colors and Inks information** lets you see the colors to be printed.

28 The **Print Settings information** shows a record of the print settings for the document.

To review the Links information:

◆ Choose Links and Images from the pop-up list at the top of the Preflight dialog box. This opens the links information **26**. *(See the exercise on page 214 for steps on how to update or relink images.)*

To review the Colors and Inks information:

◆ Choose Colors and Inks from the pop-up list at the top of the Preflight dialog box. This opens the information on the colors used within the document **27**.

To review the Print Settings information:

◆ Choose Print Settings from the pop-up list at the top of the dialog box. This shows all the print settings currently applied to the document **28**.

Creating a Preflight Report

If the Preflight command shows missing or modified links, you can use the Links and Images section to update or relink the links.

To relink or update images in the preflight report:

1. Choose the missing or modified image as shown in the Links and Images section of the Preflight dialog box **29**.

2. Choose Relink or Update. This opens the Find dialog box.

3. Navigate to find the correct image.

4. Click Choose to update the link.

TIP Choose Repair All to have InDesign automatically open the dialog box for all missing or modified links.

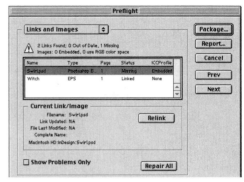

29 Use the **Links and Images** controls to update or relink modified or missing images.

Once you have run the preflight command, you can then create a text file that records all the information from the different sections of the preflight dialog box. This report can be sent along with the file to the service bureau.

To create a preflight report:

1. Run the preflight utility as described on the previous page.

2. Click Report in the Preflight dialog box.

3. Use the dialog box that opens to name and save your report.

TIP You can open the preflight report in a text editor.

Creating a Preflight Report

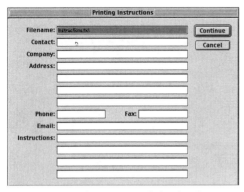

30 The **Printing Instructions dialog box** lets you enter the specific information about the file as well as contact information at your company.

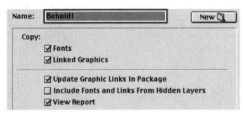

31 The **Create Package Folder dialog box** lets you choose which items should be copied to the document's folder.

Font Alert:
Restrictions apply to copying font software for use by a service provider. You are required to comply with applicable copyright law and the terms of your license agreement. For font software licensed from Adobe, your license agreement provides that you may take a copy of the font(s) you have used for a particular file to a commercial printer or other service provider, and the provider may use the font(s) to process your file, provided the provider has informed you that it has the right to use that particular software. For other font software, please obtain permission from your vendor.

32 The **Font Alert** reminds you to check the legality of sending fonts to others.

Creating a Prepress Package

A prepress package is a folder that contains all the elements necessary to print a file. For instance, in addition to the InDesign document, you may need to send placed images and fonts to the service bureau that will print your file.

To package files for printing:

1. Choose **File > Package** or click Package in the Preflight dialog box. *(See page 214.)* InDesign looks through the document and then opens the Printing Instructions dialog box **30**.

2. Fill out the contact and file information.

3. Click Continue. This opens the Create Package Folder dialog box **31**.

4. Enter a name for the folder that will hold the files.

5. Check which files you want to copy into the folder along with the InDesign document:

   • Fonts copies the fonts used in the document.

   • Linked Graphics copies placed images that are not embedded in the file.

   TIP If you choose to send fonts, a warning notice appears that reminds you about the legalities of distributing fonts **32**. *(See the sidebar on page 219 for a discussion about copying fonts.)*

6. Check Update Graphic Links in Package to make sure you have the most recent version of the graphic.

7. Check Include Fonts and Links from Hidden Layers if you have information on layers that are not visible.

8. Click View Report to launch a text editor to open the report created with the document.

9. Click Package to assemble all the necessary files in the folder.

Creating Prepress Files

Instead of sending the InDesign document to a service bureau, you can create a PostScript file that contains all the information necessary to print the file. The layout, fonts, and graphics used to create the document are combined into one file that can be set directly to a printer. This is sometimes called *printing to disk*.

A standard PostScript file contains all the information necessary to print the file as well as the specific information about the printer.

To create a standard PostScript file:

1. Choose File > Print.

2. Choose the type of printer that will print your file.

3. Set all the printing options.

TIP Check with the service bureau that will be printing your file for all the correct options. If you set any of the printing options incorrectly, the service bureau may not be able to print your file on its equipment.

4. Check Print to File (Win) **33**.

   or

   Choose File from the Destination pop-up list (Mac) **34**.

5. Choose a name and location for the file.

TIP (Mac) Add the suffix *.ps* to the file name to indicate that it is a PostScript file.

6. Click Save.

33 Check **Print to file** in the Windows Print dialog box to create a PostScript file.

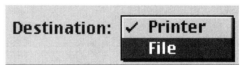

34 Choose **File** from the Macintosh Destination pop-up list in the Print dialog box to create a PostScript file.

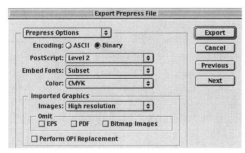

③ The **Export Prepress File** dialog box lets you set the options for a prepress file.

A prepress file contains all the information necessary to print the file but does not contain any information about the type of printer or output device. A prepress file can be printed on almost any type of device.

To create a prepress file:

1. Choose **File > Export**.

2. Choose a name and location for the file.

TIP (Mac) Add the suffix .sep to indicate that this is a prepress file.

3. Choose Prepress File from the Save As Type (Win) or Formats (Mac) pop-up list. This opens the Export Prepress File dialog box **③**.

4. Set the Prepress Options as described on the following page.

5. Choose Pages and PageMarks from the pop-up list and set those options as described on page 211.

6. Click Export.

To set the prepress options:

1. Choose ASCII or Binary from the Encoding options.

TIP Binary creates smaller files but may conflict with older systems. Use ASCII as directed by your service bureau.

2. Choose the PostScript compatibility options as follows 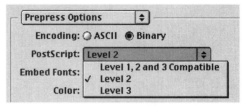:

   - If you do not know what type of device will be used, choose Level 1, 2, and 3 Compatible.

   - Choose Level 2 if you know the type of device. This can improve the speed and quality of the graphics.

   - Choose Level 3 if you know the device is Level 3.

TIP Use Level 3 only if you know the printer has a Level 3 processor.

3. Set the Embed Fonts options as follows:

   - Choose Complete to include all characters in the fonts.

   - Choose Subset to include only the characters you have used.

36 The PostScript compatibility options for a prepress file.

4. Choose the color options for your document.

TIP If your job is a process-color job, leave this setting as CMYK.

5. Choose the options for Imported Graphics:

   • Choose High Resolution if your job will be printed on a device such as an imagesetter.

   • Choose Low Resolution if your job will be printed on a desktop printer or the images will be replaced by high-resolution files.

6. Choose any of the image file types to omit from the file.

TIP Omit images only if your service bureau will be replacing those files as part of an OPI Replacement option.

7. Check Perform OPI Replacement which allows the swapping of low-resolution files with high-resolution ones. Consult your service bureau for exact instructions for how to set this up.

Copying Fonts: Legal or Not?

You may have heard stories of people carted off to prison for illegally copying software. While there have been people arrested for software piracy, the rules about fonts are more intricate.

First, most font companies, such as Adobe, allow you to send a copy of the font along with your document provided that the service bureau that is going to print your file also has its own copy of the font.

So why would a service bureau want you to send them a copy of your font if they already have a copy? This ensures that it uses exactly the same font as the one you used to create the document. However, as long as the bureau already owns a copy in its files, there is no piracy.

This is why most survice bureaus spend thousands of dollars to buy complete font libraries. If the bureau doesn't have a copy of the font, you should not send the font along with the file. Either the service bureau buys the font or you should create a prepress package.

Of course, if you use a program such as Fontographer to make your own fonts, you have total permission to copy the fonts and give them to anyone you want. For instance, all the figure numbers and the tip bullet in this book are fonts I created. I have no problem getting permission to copy those fonts.

EXPORT 13

Today there are many more options for publishing than just printed documents. After you finish your InDesign document, you may want to use it somewhere else.

For instance, you might want clients to read your document electronically—even if they don't have the InDesign application. Or you might want to take a design that you have created within InDesign and use it as part of a layout in another program. Or you may want to convert your InDesign document into Web pages.

When you convert InDesign documents into other formats, you use the export features of the program. Export refers to converting InDesign documents into other formats such as portable document format (PDF) files or Web hypertext markup language (HTML) pages.

Creating PDF Files

PDF stands for *portable document format.* You can convert your InDesign documents into PDF files that let others read the files— even if they do not have the InDesign application. In addition, you can embed within the PDF document the fonts you used in the InDesign document. This makes sure the document always looks the way it was originally created. You can also use PDF files as the format you send to the print shop or service bureau for professional printing.

To export a document as a PDF file:

1. Choose **File > Export.** The Export dialog box appears ❶.

2. Give the file a name and set the location.

3. Choose Adobe PDF from the Save as File Type (Win) or Formats (Mac) list.

4. Click Save. This opens the Export PDF dialog box where you can set the PDF settings.

5. Set the PDF Options as described on the next page.

6. Set the Compression as described on page 224.

7. Set the Pages and Page Marks as described on page 225.

8. Set the Security options as described on page 226.

9. Click Export to create the PDF file which can be sent to others.

TIP PDF files can be used for onscreen viewing or for high-resolution output. There are different settings for each of those output options.

TIP If you plan to use the PDF for high-resolution output, check with the print shop or service bureau for their exact specifications for all the PDF settings.

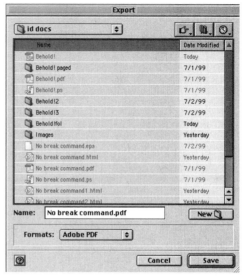

❶ The **Export dialog box** lets you choose the type of export, the name, and the location of the file.

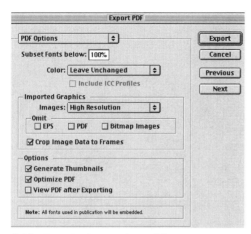

❷ The **PDF Options** settings of the Export PDF dialog box. These are the recommended settings for **high-resolution output**.

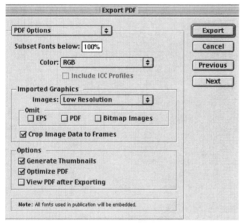

❸ The PDF Options settings recommended for onscreen viewing.

The PDF Options let you embed fonts within your document and control how the color and resolution of the file are handled.

To set the PDF Options:

1. Choose PDF Options from the pop-up list at the top of the Export PDF dialog box **❷**.

2. Set the amount for the Subset Fonts Below field. 100% includes all the characters of the font.

3. Set how to treat colors in the Color pop-up menu:

    • Leave Unchanged does not convert any of the colors in the document.

    • RGB converts all colors to RGB.

    • CMYK converts all colors to CMYK.

4. Choose High Resolution or Low Resolution for Imported Graphics from the Images pop-up menu.

    TIP Choose Low Resolution for onscreen viewing **❸**.

5. Choose which types of images, if any, you want to omit from the file.

    TIP You should not need to omit images unless you receive specific instructions from your service bureau.

6. Check Crop Image Data to Frames to limit the image information to the page.

    TIP Do not crop image data if your file has images that bleed off the page or might be needed for special positioning.

7. Set the options as follows:

    • Generate Thumbnails creates small images of each page that can be used to navigate within the PDF file.

    • Optimize PDF reduces the file size by eliminating repeating elements.

    • View PDF After Exporting automatically opens the PDF file in Adobe Acrobat to view the results.

Creating PDF Files

The compression settings can help reduce the file size of the PDF. If you create files for onscreen viewing, you will want to compress the files so they take up less space and can be transmitted quickly over the Web. However, if you create a PDF for high-resolution output, you will not want to compress the file because that will destroy some of the information in your file and cause poor quality output.

To set the compression:

1. Choose Compression from the pop-up list at the top of the Export PDF dialog box **❹**.

2. Choose the resampling options for color or grayscale images as follows:

   • Set the amount in the Downsample To field. For high-resoution output this is usually 300 DPI. For onscreen viewing this is usually 72 DPI **❺**.

   • Set the type of compression. Use Automatic for both high-resolution and onscreen viewing.

   • Set the quality setting from the pop-up list. Choose Maximim for high-resolution ouput. Choose Medium for onscreen viewing.

3. Choose the resampling options for Monochrome Bitmap Images as follows:

   • Set the amount in the Downsample To field. For high-resolution output this is usually 1200 DPI. For onscreen viewing it is usually 300 DPI.

   • Set the type of Compression from the pop-up list. CCITT Group 4 is recommended for high-resolution output. None is recommended for onscreen viewing.

4. Check Compress Text and Line Art to reduce the file size.

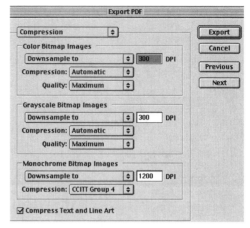

❹ The **Compression settings** of the Export PDF dialog box. These are the recommended settings for **high-resolution output.**

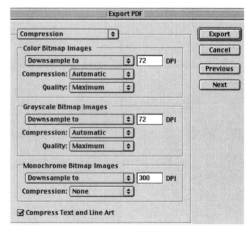

❺ The **Compression settings** recommended for onscreen viewing.

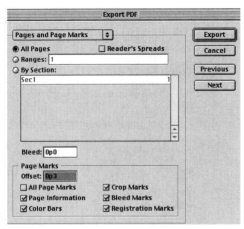

⊙ The **Pages and Page Marks options** of the Export PDF dialog box.

The Pages and Page Marks settings let you choose which pages to export. These settings also let you set whether any special information (sometimes called *printer's marks*) should be added around the page.

To set the Pages and Page Marks:

1. Choose Pages and Page Marks from the pop-up list at the top of the Export PDF dialog box. This opens the Pages and Page Marks options **⊙**.

2. Set the pages as described on page 207.

3. Check Reader's Spreads to export the pages in a spread next to each other as they would appear when bound in a publication.

TIP Do not select Reader's Spreads for professional print publishing. The service bureau cannot separate Reader's Spread pages for imposition.

4. Set the bleed amount.

5. Set the page marks as described on page 211.

You can also set security options for PDF files. For instance, you may want to set a password so that only certain people can open the file. You can also determine what other people can do with the file once it is opened.

To set the Security options:

1. Choose Security from the pop-up list at the top of the Export PDF dialog box ➐.

2. Check Use Security Features to turn on the security options.

3. Type a password in the Open Document field to limit who can open the document to those who know the password.

4. Type a password in the Change Security field to limit who can change the security options once the PDF is open.

5. Check which actions you do not want to allow:

   • Printing disallows the Print command.

   • Changing the Document keeps anyone from changing text in the document.

   • Copying Text and Graphics prevents anyone from copying the text or images for use elsewhere.

   • Adding or Changing Notes and Form Fields keeps anyone from adding Acrobat annotations and comments.

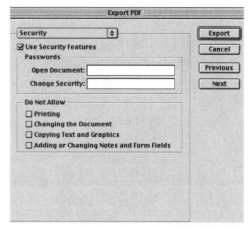

➐ The **Security options** of the Export PDF dialog box let you control what others can do when they open the PDF.

Creating EPS Files

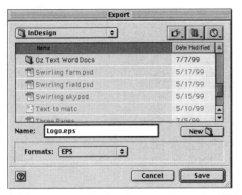

❽ The **Export dialog box** lets you choose the EPS format to save as an Encapsulated PostScript file.

You might create a special shape or design in InDesign that you would like to use in other page-layout programs or as part of a Photoshop or Illustrator file. Export the file as an EPS, or *Encapsulated PostScript,* file so that you can use it in other applications.

To create an EPS file:

1. Choose **File** > **Export.** The Export dialog box appears **❽**.

2. Give the file a name and set the location.

3. Choose EPS from the Save As File Type (Win) or Formats (Mac) pop-up list.

4. Click Save. This opens the Export EPS dialog box.

5. Set the EPS Options as described in the next exercise.

6. Choose Pages from the pop-up list and set those options as described on the following page.

7. Click Export to create the EPS file which can then be used as a graphic in other files.

To set the EPS Options:

1. Choose EPS Options from the pop-up list at the top of the Export EPS dialog box. This displays the EPS Options **⑨**.

2. Choose either ASCII or Binary from the Encoding choices.

TIP Use Binary unless you are using a PC network that requires ASCII data.

3. Choose the PostScript options:

   • If you do not know what type of device will be used, choose Level 1, 2, and 3 Compatible.

   • Choose Level 2 if you know the type of device. This can improve the speed and quality of the graphics.

   • Choose Level 3 only if you know the device is Level 3.

4. Set the Embed Fonts options:

   • Choose Complete to include all characters in the fonts.

   • Choose Subset to include only the characters you have used.

4. Choose the color options for your document.

5. Choose the options for Imported Graphics:

   • Choose High Resolution if your job will be printed on a imagesetter.

   • Choose Low Resolution if your job will be printed on a desktop printer.

6. Choose the file types to omit.

TIP Omit images only if your service bureau will be replacing those files as part of an OPI Replacement option.

7. Check Perform OPI Replacement which swaps low-resolution files with high-resolution ones. Consult your service bureau for how to set this up.

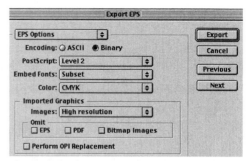

⑨ The **Export EPS options** for an Encapsulated PostScript file.

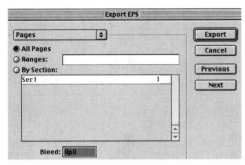

⑩ The **Pages options** for an Encapsulated PostScript file.

To set the Pages options:

1. Choose Pages from the pop-up list at the top of the Export EPS dialog box. This displays the Pages options **⑩**.

2. Choose the pages to print as follows:

   - All Pages outputs all the pages in the document.

   - Ranges let you specify certain pages. Use a hyphen to specify a range of pages, such as 4–6. Use a comma to specify individual pages, such as 8, 9.

   - By Section exports specific sections of a document. *(For more information on creating sections, see Chapter 8, "Long Documents.")*

   TIP You can combine ranges and individual pages in one field.

   TIP Each page creates a separate EPS file.

3. Set the amount of bleed in the Bleed field.

   TIP A bleed is the amount that images can extend outside the page size.

Creating EPS Files

Creating Web Files

Although most people use InDesign to create printed materials, you may also want to use your designs as Web pages. The format for Web pages is a text file marked up with coding tags from a language called HTML *(hypertext markup language)*. Fortunately, it is rather easy to change InDesign documents from print layouts to HTML pages ⓫. If you need more information on creating documents for the Web, see *The Non-Designer's Web Book* by Robin Williams and John Tollett, published by Peachpit Press.

TIP Use InDesign's HTML export only for basic Web page creation. To create intricate Web sites, you should use an HTML editor such as Adobe GoLive or Macromedia Dreamweaver.

⓫ InDesign lets you convert InDesign documents from print layouts to HTML pages.

To create HTML files:

1. Choose **File>Export.** The Export dialog box appears.

2. Give the file a name and set the location.

3. Choose HTML from the Save As File Type (Win) or Formats (Mac) pop-up list.

4. Click Save. This opens the Export HTML dialog box.

5. Set the document options as described on the following page.

6. Set the formatting options as described on page 232.

7. Set the layout options as described on page 233.

8. Set the graphics options as described on page 234.

9. Click Export to create the HTML files. These can be added to the server that holds a Web site.

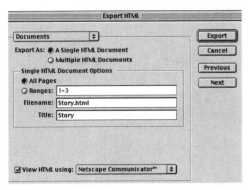

⑫ The **Documents options** control the pages to be exported as HTML files.

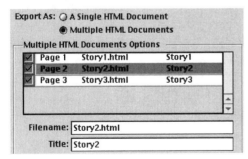

⑬ The **Single HTML Document Options** let you control how multiple pages are converted into a single HTML document.

⑭ The **Multiple HTML Documents Options** let you choose which pages should be exported as HTML documents.

Unlike print pages that are a fixed size, Web pages can expand in length. So you have a choice as to how to convert the print layout into Web pages.

To set the Documents options:

1. Choose Documents from the pop-up list at the top of the Export HTML dialog box. This opens the Documents options **⑫**.

2. Choose Export As A Single HTML Document to convert multiple pages into one HTML page.

   or

   Choose Export As Multiple HTML Documents to convert each InDesign page into its own HTML page.

TIP If you export multiple pages as a single HTML document, a horizontal line is inserted between the pages in the Web browser.

3. If you choose Single HTML Document, choose All Pages or a range of page **⑬**.

4. If you choose Multiple HTML Documents, use the Multiple HTML Documents Options **⑭** to choose which of the pages should be exported for the current HTML document.

5. Set the file name and title for each Web page in the appropriate fields.

6. Check View HTML Using and set the browser you want to use to preview the pages.

Creating Web Files

231

Web pages have different formats than print layouts. For instance, you may want to change the text color so that it is easier to read. You may also want to set a specific background color or image.

To set the Formatting options:

1. Choose Formatting from the pop-up list at the top of the Export HTML dialog box. This opens the Formatting options 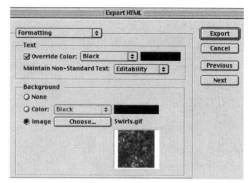.

2. Check Override Color to choose a color for the text on the Web page.

3. Choose the Background options as follows:

   • None leaves the background as set in the InDesign layout.

   • Color allows you to set a color for the background of all the pages.

   • Image allows you to choose a GIF or JPEG image that will be repeated as a pattern on all the Web pages .

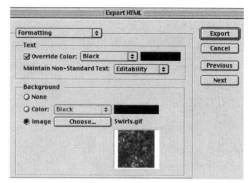

🔟 The **Formatting options** control the text and background colors of the exported HTML files.

🔟 The **Background Image option** allows you to set an image to repeat across the Web page.

⑰ The **Layout options** control the text, margins, and navigation elements of the Web pages.

CSS-1 option

None

⑱ The **CSS-1 option** maintains a close approximation of the printed layout. The **None option** can cause text and graphics to become separated.

⑲ The **Navigation Bar option** adds text links that can be used to move to the next or previous pages.

When you convert a print document to HTML, you also have choices as to how the layout of the page is converted.

To set the Layout options:

1. Choose Layout from the pop-up list at the top of the Export HTML dialog box. This opens the Layout options **⑰**.

2. Choose the Positioning options as follows:

   • Best (CSS-1) uses cascading style sheets to create the closest version of the layout.

TIP CSS-1 requires Netscape or Microsoft browser versions 4.0 or later for proper viewing **⑱**.

   • None assembles the pages with text and graphics in separate paragraphs.

3. Choose the InDesign Margins options as follows:

   • Maintain keeps an area around the page that corresponds to the margins.

   • None removes the area for the margins.

4. Choose the Navigation Bar options as follows:

   • Top, Bottom, or Both add navigational links to the top or bottom of the Web page. These links, labeled <PrevNext> allow you to move from one Web page to another **⑲**.

   • None adds no links to the pages.

TIP The navigational links are added only if you have a multipage document that is set for Multiple HTML Documents options *(see page 231)*.

Creating Web Files

When you convert InDesign documents to HTML, there are many elements, such as placed images, frame strokes and fills, and lines that need to be converted into images. The Graphics options control how those objects are converted.

To set the Graphics options:

1. Choose Graphics from the pop-up list at the top of the Export HTML dialog box. This opens the Graphics options **20**.

2. Choose the Save Images As options as follows:

   - Automatic lets InDesign choose which type of image, GIF or JPEG, should be used.

   - GIF forces all images to the GIF format, which is usually better for flat art.

   - JPEG forces all images to the JPEG format, which is usually better for photographic images.

3. Check Use Images Sub-Folder to place the images in a folder labeled Images.

4. Set the GIF Settings Palette as follows:

   - Adaptive (no dither) creates a representative sample of colors. These colors may or may not include Web-safe colors.

   - Web limits the colors to the 216 Web-safe colors that are present in both the Macintosh and Windows operating systems. This option avoids dithering colors when pages are viewed on a monitor that can only display 256 colors.

   - System (Win) or System (Mac) limits the colors to the built-in colors for the designated computer system. This option is useful if your pages will be viewed only by users of one type of computer, perhaps as part of a company's internal Web site, sometimes called an *intranet*.

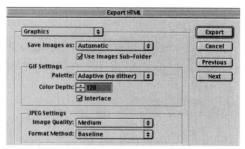

20 The **Graphics options** control how non-text items are converted into images.

21 An example of how an **interlaced GIF** or **baseline JPEG** image appear.

- Exact uses only those colors that are exactly in the graphic. If there are more than 256 colors in the graphic, InDesign displays a warning that the exact match is not possible.

5. If you choose Adaptive or Exact, set the GIF Settings Color Depth to the number of colors. Lower numbers create smaller files but can change the appearance of the image.

6. Check Interlace to create an image that appears gradually on the page **21**.

7. Choose Low, Medium, High, or Maximum from the JPEG Settings Image Quality list. The lower the quality, the smaller the file size.

8. Choose a JPEG Settings Format Method as follows:

- Progressive creates an image that appears gradually on the page. This is similar to the Interlaced GIF.

- Baseline creates an image that appears all at once, after the entire image has been downloaded.

Exporting Text

You may find it necessary to export text from InDesign. For instance, you may want to send the text to someone who works with Microsoft Word. You can send them a text file by exporting the text.

To export text:

1. Place an insertion point inside the frame that contains the text. All the text within that frame will be exported.

TIP Select an area of text to export only that portion of the text.

2. Choose **File > Export.** This opens the Export dialog box.

3. Use the Formats pop-up list **22** to choose what type of text should be exported:

   - Rich Text Format keeps all the styles and text formatting. This format can be opened by most word processors, especially Microsoft Word.

   - Text-only exports only the characters of the text and discards any styles and text formatting. Use this option only if you want to strip out the text formatting or the application you are working with does not support the Rich Text Format.

4. Name the file and choose a destination.

5. Click Save to export the file.

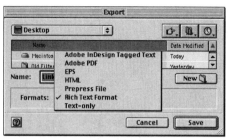

22 The **Export Formats pop-up list** lets you choose the format for text exported from InDesign.

Exporting Text

CUSTOMIZING INDESIGN 14

Designers and art directors are not followers. They are leaders, innovators—the ones that break away from the pack and forge their own identities. So, it is little wonder that they don't want to use software the same way the engineers designed it. The want their programs to work the way they want to work.

The InDesign team recognized that need for individuation and gave you many different ways to customize the program. You can customize the keyboard shortcuts so that they are similar to other software you use. You can change settings for the displays of images and onscreen elements. You can even automatically update the software so that it is always current.

It's all your choice. You're InControl of InDesign!

Modifying Keyboard Shortcuts

Keyboard shortcuts are the fastest way to invoke commands. InDesign has many keyboard shortcuts for applying commands, choosing tools, and displaying palettes.

InDesign groups shortcuts into sets. The program ships with two sets of shortcuts. The default set uses most of the shortcuts found in Adobe products such as Illustrator or Photoshop. The other set contains the shortcuts used in QuarkXPress 4.0.

To choose the QuarkXPress shortcut set:

1. Choose File>Edit Shortcuts. The Edit Shortcuts dialog box appears ❶.

2. Choose Set for QuarkXPress 4.0 from the Set pop-up list.

3. Click OK. The new shortcuts appear in the menus ❷.

TIP Some shortcuts do not change. For instance, the Zoom tool does not change to the Control key (Mac) or Ctrl-Spacebar (Win) shortcuts.

If you work with other progrms such as Macromedia FreeHand, you may want to create your own shortcut set.

To create a new shortcut set:

1. Choose File>Edit Shortcuts.

2. Choose New Set. This opens the New Set dialog box ❸.

3. Enter a name for the set.

4. Choose a set that the new set will be based on.

TIP Sets must be based on another set so that it starts with some shortcuts. However, if you later change something in the original set, the one that was based on it does not change.

5. Click OK. You can now edit the set as described on the next page.

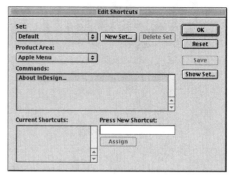

❶ The **Edit Shortcuts** dialog box lets you change the shortcuts used for commands, tools, and palettes.

❷ Changing the InDesign shortcuts to the set for QuarkXPress 4.0 changes commands, such as Place becomes Cmd/Ctrl-E rather than Cmd/Ctrl-D.

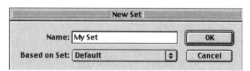

❸ The **New Set** dialog box lets you name a new shortcut set and choose which set it should be based on.

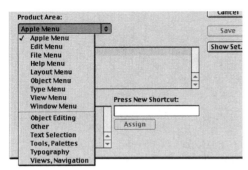

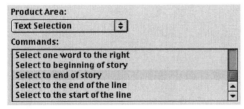

❹ The **Product Area** pop-up list contains all the areas of the program that have shortcuts that can be modified.

❺ The specific commands are listed for each product area.

Current Shortcuts: **Press New Shortcut:**

❻ New keystrokes appear in the **Press New Shortcut** field.

To change a shortcut:

1. Choose a shortcut set in the Edit Shortcuts dialog box or start a new set.

TIP You cannot change the Default or Quark XPress sets.

2. Choose which part of the program you want to change in the Product Area pop-up list ❹.

3. Choose a command from the commands under the Product Area list ❺.

4. Press the keys on the keyboard that you want to assign to invoke the command. The keys appear in the Press New Shortcut field ❻.

TIP If the keystroke is already assigned to another command, the command that uses the shortcut is listed in the Currently Assigned To area.

5. Change the keys if necessary by selecting them and typing a new combination.

6. Click Assign to change the shortcut.

7. Make any other changes you want.

8. Click Save to save the set as changed.

To delete a set:

1. Choose File > Edit Shortcuts.

2. Use the pop-up list to choose the set.

3. Click Delete Set.

You can also print out the list of the keystrokes in a set.

To print a shortcut set:

1. Choose File > Edit Shortcuts.

2. Use the pop-up list to choose the set.

3. Click Show Set. This opens the Simple Text (Mac) or Notepad (Win) application which displays the shortcuts as a text file.

4. Print the text file.

Modifying Keyboard Shortcuts

Setting the General Preferences

You can also set the preferences for how you work with InDesign. For instance, you can change how images and page numbers are displayed in the General Preferences.

To set the general preferences:

1. Choose File > Preferences > General. This opens the Preferences dialog box with the general options visible ❼.

2. Set the options for how images are displayed with the Images Display pop-up list. *(For more information on working with images, see Chapter 7, "Imported Graphics.")*

3. Set the options for how page numbers are displayed with the Page Numbering View pop-up list. *(For more information on working with page numbers, see Chapter 8, "Long Documents.")*

4. Choose Show Tool Tips to display the small labels that tell the names of tools and features.

5. Choose Overprint Black to have all black ink automatically overprint any other colors it passes over. *(For more information on preparing a file for printing, see Chapter 12, "Output.")*

TIP Use the Preferences pop-up list at the top of the dialog box or use the Prev (previous) and Next buttons to move to any of the other preference settings.

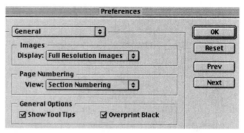

❼ The **General Preferences** settings of the Preferences dialog box.

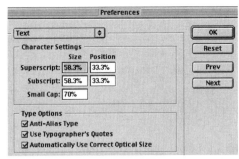

⑧ The **Text Preferences** settings of the Preferences dialog box.

Off

Dor

On

Dor

⑨ An example of what the **Anti-Alias Type** setting does to text.

"The Wizard of Oz" Off

"The Wizard of Oz" On

⑩ An example of using typographer's quotes.

Setting the Text Preferences

You can also set the preferences for how the text is displayed and formatted. These are the Text Preferences.

To set the text preferences:

1. Choose **File** > **Preferences** > **Text**. This opens the Preferences dialog box **⑧** with the Text options visible.

2. Set each of the controls for the size and position of the superscript, subscript, and small caps characters. *(For more information on working with text, see Chapter 3, "Text.")*

3. Check Anti-Alias Type to add a soft edge to the type displayed on the monitor **⑨**. This may make the type look better onscreen, but it does not affect the final output of the page.

4. Check Use Typographer's Quotes to automatically change typewriter quotes into the proper open-and-close, curly quote characters **⑩**.

TIP These are called Smart Quotes in many other applications.

TIP You may want to turn off Smart Quotes or convert them into straight quotes if you export your documents to the Web. Smart Quotes characters may not display correctly when viewed by different browsers on different platforms.

5. Check Automatically Use Correct Optical Size to set the correct value for the optical size of multiple master fonts.

Setting Composition Preferences

You can set the preferences for how text is composed and if violations of the composition settings are displayed.

To set the composition preferences:

1. Choose File > Preferences > Composition. This opens the Preferences dialog box ⓫ with the Composition options visible.

2. Set the controls for the Adobe Multi-line Composer. *(For more information on composing text, see Chapter 10, "Advanced Text.")*

3. Choose the Highlight options as follows:

   • Keep Violations highlights lines that have been broken in violation of the Keep With settings you have chosen for the paragraph options.

   • H&J Violations highlights those areas that have been set in violation of the hyphenation or justification controls ⓬.

   ⓣ H&J violations occur when there is no other way to set the text except to break the H&J controls.

   • Substituted Fonts highlights those characters that are substituted for a font that is not installed in the computer system.

   ⓣ If the shape of the uninstalled font exists in the Adobe Type Manager database, the shape of the font is approximated. If not, a default font is used.

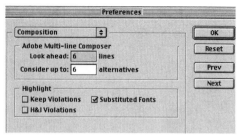

⓫ The **Composition Preferences** settings of the Preferences dialog box.

She walked across the yellow bricks one by one. She started slowly at first, but then started to walk faster as she gathered courage.

⓬ The highlighted text shows that the space between the words is an **H&J Violation.**

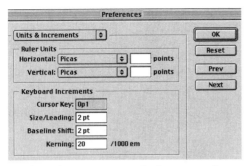

 The Units & Increments Preferences settings of the Preferences dialog box.

Setting the Units and Increments Preferences

You can also set the preferences for what measurement units InDesign uses and the increments that settings are changed using the keyboard shortcuts. These are the Units and Increments Preferences.

To set the units and increments preferences:

1. Choose File > Preferences > Units & Increments. This opens the Preferences dialog box with the Units & Increments options visible.

2. Choose a unit of measurement for the Horizontal and Vertical Ruler Units.

3. In the Cursor Key field, choose the amount that the arrow keys should nudge objects.

4. In the Size/Leading field, choose the amount that the type size and leading should be increased by the keyboard shortcuts.

5. In the Baseline Shift field, choose the amount that the baseline shift should change by the keyboard shortcut.

6. In the Kerning field, choose the amount that the kerning should be changed by the keyboard shortcut.

Setting the Units and Increments Preferences

Setting the Grids Preferences

InDesign lets you change the colors and increments of the baseline and document grids. *(For more information on setting the grids preferences, see Chapter 2, "Document Setup.")*

To set the Baseline Grid preferences:

1. Choose File > Preferences > Grids. This opens the Preferences dialog box ⑭ with the Grids options visible.

2. Choose the Baseline Grid options as follows:

   • Choose the color from the Color pop-up list.

   • Enter a value in the Start field to position where the grid should start on the page.

   • Enter a value in the Increment Every field to set the distance between the lines of the grid.

   • Set an amount in the View Threshold field to set the lowest magnification that the grid is visible at.

To set the Document Grid preferences:

1. Choose File > Preferences > Grids.

2. Choose Document Grid options as follows:

   • Choose the color from the Color pop-up list.

   • Enter a value in the Grid field to set the size of the grid.

   • Enter a value in the Subdivisions field to set the distance between the lines of the grid.

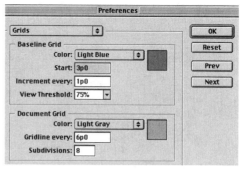

⑭ The **Grids Preferences** settings of the Preferences dialog box.

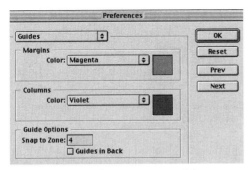

 The **Guides Preferences** settings of the Preferences dialog box.

Setting the Guides Preferences

InDesign lets you change the colors behavior of the margin and column guides. *(For more information on setting the guides preferences, see Chapter 2, "Document Setup.")*

To set the guides preferences:

1. Choose **File**>**Preferences**>**Guides**. This opens the Preferences dialog box ⓑ with the Guides options visible.

2. Set the color for the margin guides.

3. Set the color for the column guides.

4. In the Snap To Zone fielde, set the how close objects should be so they snap to guides. This amount is set in pixels.

5. Check Guides in Back to position the guides behind objects.

Setting the Dictionary Preferences

InDesign lets you choose the default dictionary and the hyphenation controls. These are the Dictionary Preferences. *(For more information on setting the dictionary for a document, see Chapter 9, "Automating Text." For more information on working with hyphenation, see Chapter 10, "Advanced Text.")*

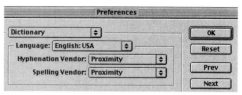

⓰ The **Dictionary Preferences** settings of the Preferences dialog box.

To set the dictionary preferences:

1. Choose **File** > **Preferences** > **Dictionary**. This opens the Preferences dialog box **⓰** with the Dictionary options visible.

2. Set the default language by using the Language pop-up list.

3. If you have installed special hyphenation preferences, choose a preference from the Hyphenation Vendor pop-up list.

4. If you have installed special spelling preferences, choose a preference from the Spelling Vendor pop-up list.

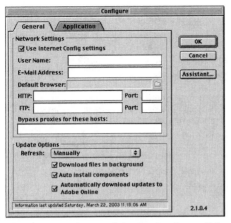

 The **General controls** in the Configure dialog box for the Adobe Online settings.

Updating with Adobe Online

One of the benefits of using InDesign is that it is entirely modular. This means that Adobe can send out updates or replacements to various parts of the program via the Internet. You use the Adobe Online application controls to set up how these updates are received.

To set the general online controls:

1. Choose **File** > **Preferences** > **Online Settings.** This opens the Configure dialog box for the online settings.

2. Click the General tab to display the general settings ⑰.

3. Check Use Internet Config Settings.

4. Fill out the Network Settings fields for how your computer connects to the Internet. These are the settings provided by your Internet service provider.

5. Choose how often you want to update from the Refresh pop-up list:

   • Manually lets you dial up yourself.

   • Once a Day, Once a Week, or Once a Month automatically connects to Adobe Online.

   TIP If you use a dial-up modem, update manually. If you have a permanent connection to the Internet, you can set the update to happen automatically.

6. Check Download File In Background to have the file download while you do other work.

7. Check Auto Install Components to have the new features automatically replace older files.

8. Check Automatically Download Updates to Adobe Online to update the Adobe Online application itself.

You can also set the controls for what information you get when connected to Adobe Online.

To set the application online controls:

1. Choose File > Preferences > Online Settings.

2. Click the Application tab to display the application settings 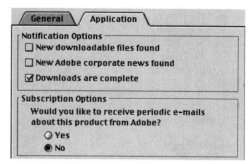.

3. Check the Notification Options to let you know what changes have been made by Adobe Online.

4. Check the Subscription Options to set Adobe Online to send you automatic e-mails of updates to InDesign.

TIP The e-mail subscription is recommended if you have a dial-up modem and do not automatically receive updates to InDesign.

® The **Application controls** for the Adobe Online settings.

Updating with Adobe Online

COMPARED TO QUARKXPRESS 15

Most people who learn a page-layout program such as InDesign are actually learning two things: using a page-layout program as well as the specifics of the application. The release of InDesign is slightly different.

Adobe expects many people who are experienced with QuarkXPress to switch to InDesign. Those new users don't need to learn about using a page layout program—they already know QuarkXPress. They need to focus just on the specifics of InDesign and how they compare to QuarkXPress.

This chapter lets you compare Adobe InDesign to QuarkXPress 4. If you are familiar with QuarkXPress you can use this chapter as a super quickstart to using InDesign. If you need more information, you can refer to the previous chapters for the exercises.

Please note that although there are some QuarkXPress features that you won't find in InDesign, this chapter doesn't cover the many powerful features found in InDesign that aren't in QuarkXPress. Also, features that are extremely similar, such as copy, cut, and paste, are not listed in this chapter.

TIP Each of the figures in this chapter displays the InDesign items on the left and the QuarkXPress items on the right.

Working with Tools

Most of the tools in QuarkXPress have direct counterparts in InDesign. The only big differences are found in the selection tool and linking.

Item Tool

- InDesign's Selection tool is most similar to the QuarkXPress Item tool ❶. Both move objects and change the size of bounding boxes. *(See page 64.)*

Content Tool

- For graphics inside frames, InDesign's Direct Selection tool is somewhat similar to the QuarkXPress Content tool ❷. The Direct Selection tool allows you to move a graphic within a frame. *(See page 121.)*

- For text frames, InDesign's Text tool takes the role of the QuarkXPress Content tool ❸. The Text tool is used to select text within a frame. The Text tool can also be used to draw a text frame. *(See page 40.)*

❶ The InDesign Selection tool is most similar to the QuarkXPress Item tool.

❷ The InDesign Direct Selection tool lets you move graphics inside frames. This is similar to the QuarkXPress Content tool.

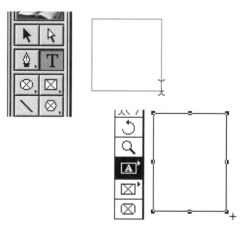

❸ For text frames, InDesign's Text tool takes the role of the QuarkXPress Content tool.

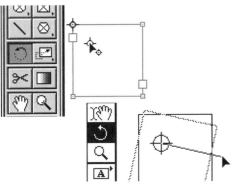

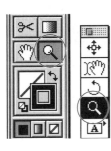

❹ InDesign's Rotation tool requires a two-step process, unlike the simple drag in QuarkXPress.

❺ The Zoom tools in both programs are almost identical in their operation.

❻ The Hand tool can be chosen as a tool in InDesign or by using keyboard shortcuts. In QuarkXPress it is accessed only by keyboard shortcuts.

Rotation Tool

- InDesign's Rotation tool is very similar to the QuarkXPress Rotation tool ❹. The major difference is that you must first position the point of rotation in InDesign rather than just drag as in QuarkXPress. *(See page 66.)*

Zoom Tool

- While the two tools are virtually identical in their operation ❺, the keyboard shortcuts are very different in InDesign. Press Cmd/Ctrl-Spacebar to access the Zoom tool. Add the Opt/Alt to zoom out. There is no preference to set how much each click changes the magnification. However, InDesign does allow much greater magnification amounts. *(See page 31.)*

Hand (Grabber) Tool

- Unlike QuarkXPress, InDesign places the Hand tool in the Toolbox. While the two tools work the same way, the keyboard shortcuts are very different. The InDesign shortcut for the Hand tool is to press the Spacebar. However, if you are working with text inside a frame, the shortcut is to press the Opt/Alt key and then press the mouse to access the Hand tool ❻. *(See page 32.)*

Working with Tools

Text box Tools

- There are no specific text boxes in InDesign. Any frame can hold text or graphics **❼**. *(See page 60.)*

Picture box Tools

- There are graphic frames that display the crossed lines familiar to QuarkXPress users **❽**. However, these frames can be converted to text frames by simply importing text or clicking with the Text tool. *(See page 41.)*

Line Tools

- There is only one type of line tool in InDesign **❾**. Use the Shift key to constrain the lines to the orthogonal lines found in QuarkXPress. *(See page 61.)*

Text on a Path Tools

- InDesign does not support text on a path **❿**.

Text Link Tools

- There are no specific linking tools. Either of the selection tools can be used to link text from one frame to another **⓫**. *(See page 56.)*

Tool Behavior

- Unlike QuarkXPress, InDesign does not switch back to the selection tools after you draw an object. The tool remains selected until you choose a new tool.

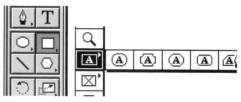

❼ InDesign's Unassigned frames can hold text or graphics. QuarkXPress has specific text boxes.

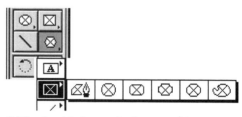

❽ The Graphic frames display crossed lines but can hold graphics or text.

❾ InDesign's Line tool draws both angled and well as orthogonal lines.

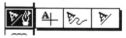

❿ There is no equivalent to the QuarkXPress text on a path.

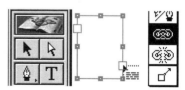

⓫ Instead of the QuarkXPress Link tools, you use the selection tools in InDesign to link text frames.

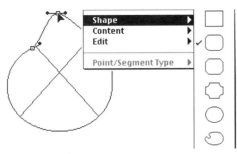

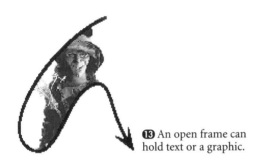

⓬ With InDesign you change the shape of a frame manually with the Pen and selection tools.

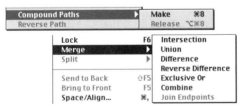

⓭ An open frame can hold text or a graphic.

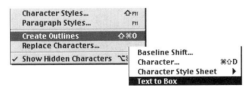

⓮ Compound paths in InDesign are the equivalent of the QuarkXPress Combine command.

Working with Boxes

There are a few differences in how you work with boxes, or frames, in InDesign.

Box Shapes

- All frames in InDesign can be turned into other shapes by adding points with the Pen tool. There are no specific polygon, elliptical, or rectangular shapes in InDesign. There are no commands to change one shape into another **⓬**.

- Unlike the closed boxes in QuarkXPress, InDesign's frames do not have to be closed paths to hold text or graphics **⓭**.

Merge Boxes

- Although InDesign does not have all of the QuarkXPress Merge commands, the Compound paths in QuarkXPress are similar to the Combine command in InDesign **⓮**.

Text to Box

- The InDesign Create Outlines command replicates the QuarkXPress Text to Box command **⓯**.

⓯ The Create Outlines command in InDesign is the equivalent of the QuarkXPress Text to Box command.

Creating a Layout

There are some important differences in the document layout between QuarkXPress and InDesign.

Document Layout Palette

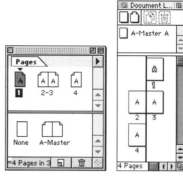

- InDesign's Pages palette corresponds to the QuarkXPress Document Layout palette ⓰. *(See page 134.)*

- The New pages and Master pages icons are located at the bottom of InDesign's Pages palette.

- The Delete page icon is located at the bottom of the Pages palette.

- There is no spine to indicate left and right facing pages.

- You can resize InDesign's Pages palette to be more similar to the QuarkXPress Document Layout palette ⓱.

- Use InDesign's Navigator palette to also mimic the QuarkXPress Document Layout palette ⓲.

⓰ InDesign's Pages palette corresponds to the QuarkXPress Document Layout palette.

Multipage Spreads

- In QuarkXPress, multiple pages can be dragged next to each other to create multipage spreads. In InDesign, these spreads are called *island spreads* ⓳. *(See page 137.)*

⓱ You can resize InDesign's Pages palette to resemble the QuarkXPress Document Layout palette.

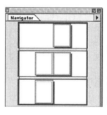

⓲ The Navigator palette also resembles the Document Layout palette, but it displays the actual information on the pages.

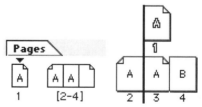

⓳ Create an island spread in InDesign to duplicate the multipage spreads in QuarkXPress.

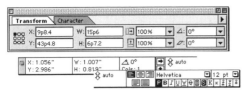

⓴ Use a combination of the Transform and Character palettes to duplicate the QuarkXPress Measurements palette for text boxes.

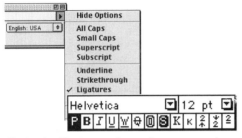

㉑ Use the Character palette submenu to apply character styles.

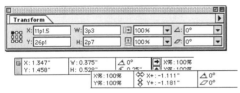

㉒ The InDesign Transform palette performs the functions of both sides of the Measurements palette for picture boxes.

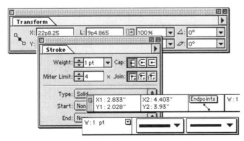

㉓ The Measurements palette for lines is duplicated in InDesign by a combination of the Transform and Stroke palettes.

Finding the Measurements Palette

The QuarkXPress Measurements palette changes depending on the type of object selected. InDesign uses several separate palettes to duplicate those functions.

Text measurements palette

- Assemble the Transform and Character palettes together to duplicate the QuarkXPress Measurements palette for text objects **⓴**.

- When the object is selected with the Selection tool, the Transform palette is visible.

- When the text is selected, the Character palette is visible.

- The character styles are found in the submenu of the Character palette **㉑**.

Picture measurements palette

- The Transform palette serves the function of both sides of the QuarkXPress Measurements palette **㉒**.

- When selected with the Selection tool, the Transform palette displays the frame information, much like the left side of the Measurements palette.

- When selected with the Direct Selection tool, the Transform palette displays the graphic information, or right side of the Measurements palette.

Line measurements palette

- The Transform palette displays the information for the left side of the Measurements palette when a line is chosen **㉓**.

- The right side of the Measurements palette is duplicated by the Stroke palette.

Creating Colors and Blends

Working with colors is very similar in the two programs.

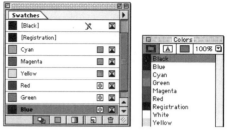

Defining Colors

- The QuarkXPress Colors list is the equivalent of InDesign's Swatches palette ㉔. *(See page 97.)*

TIP Try to avoid using InDesign's Color palette. This produces unnamed colors within the document that can cause problems later if you need to change those colors globally. *(See page 104.)*

㉔ Use the InDesign Swatches palette as the equivalent of the QuarkXPress Colors list.

Color Models

- Pantone colors and the other color models are found in InDesign's Swatches libraries ㉕. *(See page 102.)*

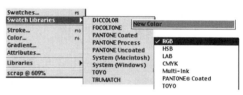

㉕ The color models, such as the Pantone colors, are found in the InDesign Swatches Libraries.

Tints

- Tints of swatches can be made from the Color palette. They can then be applied to objects ㉖. *(See page 103.)*

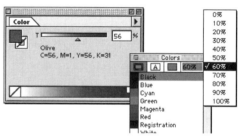

Defining Gradients

- InDesign's gradients are similar to the QuarkXPress blends ㉗.

- Use multiple colors in the gradient to replicate the QuarkXPress midlinear blend. *(See page 105.)*

㉖ Tints are created from named colors in InDesign.

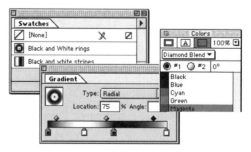

㉗ InDesign gradients can create some of the same effects as QuarkXPress blends.

Creating Colors and Blends

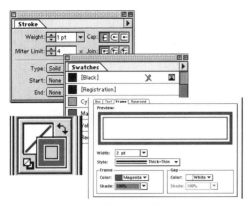

28 The frame controls in QuarkXPress are duplicated by the Toolbox, Swatches palette, and Stroke palette in InDesign.

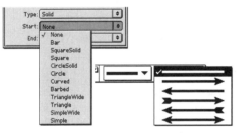

29 Use the InDesign Stroke palette to format arrow heads.

Creating Frames and Rules

In QuarkXPress, frames are the special effects applied to the edge of boxes. Frames are called strokes in InDesign. *(See page 77.)*

Applying Frames

- Use the Toolbox or Color palette to set the color for a frame **28**.

- Use the Stroke palette to set the stroke width.

Formatting Frames

- InDesign does not let you create striped frames.

- InDesign does not let you control the gap color.

Ends for Rules

- Arrowheads are applied using the Stroke palette **29**. *(See page 79.)*

Runarounds and Clipping Paths

Several features of QuarkXPress are different in InDesign when it comes to runarounds and clipping paths.

Applying a Runaround

- To run text around a graphic or object, use the Text Wrap command ③⓪. *(See page 192.)*

- There is no equivalent of the Auto Image runaround.

Creating Clipping Paths

- Use the Clipping Path dialog box to create a clipping path from the white spaces of an image ③①. *(See page 129.)*

- Clipping paths cannot be created from alpha channels.

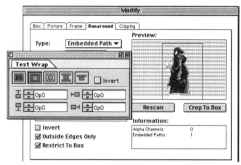

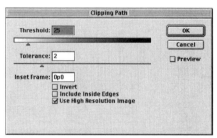

③⓪ The Text Wrap palette performs the same functions as the QuarkXPress Runaround dialog box.

③① Frames that act as clipping paths can be created in InDesign with the Clipping Path dialog box.

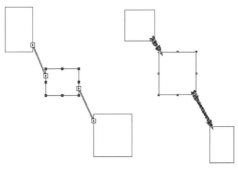

32 The InDesign Show Text Threads command is the equivalent of using the Links tool in QuarkXPress.

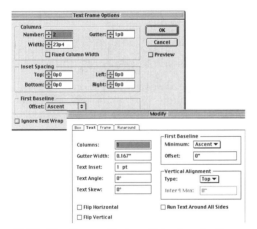

33 The Text Frames Options dialog box duplicates the QuarkXPress options for text boxes.

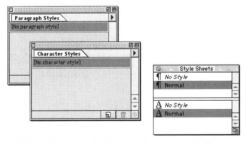

34 The Character Styles and Paragraph Styles palettes in InDesign duplicate the QuarkXPress Style Sheets.

Working with Text

Most of the text features in QuarkXPress are found in InDesign. However, they are located in different places.

Text Links

- The links between text frames are seen by choosing **View > Show Text Threads 32**. *(See page 56.)*

Text Columns

- The columns within a text box are controlled by choosing **Object > Text Frame Options 33**. *(See page 57.)*

Styles

- The QuarkXPress Style Sheets palette is duplicated by InDesign's Paragraph Styles and Character Styles palettes **34**. *(See page 168.)*

Working with Text

Paragraph Rules

- The QuarkXPress Paragraph Rules are found as part of the Rules settings of the Paragraph palette submenu **35**. *(See page 189.)*

H&J Settings

- The QuarkXPress H&J settings are found as part of the Hyphenation settings of the Paragraph palette submenu **36**. *(See page 182.)*

Invisibles

- Choose **Type > Show Hidden Characters** to see the Invisibles **37**. *(See page 55.)*

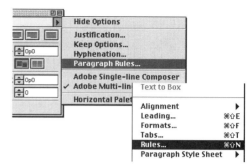

35 Paragraph rules are found in the submenu of the Paragraph palette.

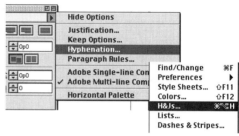

36 H&J controls are found in the submenu of the Paragraph palette.

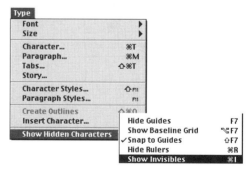

37 The QuarkXPress Invisibles are called Hidden Characters in InDesign.

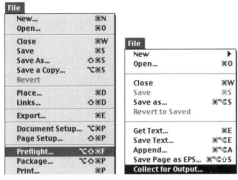

❸❽ The features of Collect for Output are contained in the Preflight and Package commands.

Outputting Files

While InDesign has many additional output options, there are some similarities to QuarkXPress.

Collect for Output

- The QuarkXPress Collect for Output feature is found as a combination of the Preflight and Package commands **❸❽**. (See pages 212 and 215.)

Font Usage

- Font usage is found as part of the Preflight package **❸❾**.

Picture Usage

- Picture usage is found as part of the Preflight package and the Links palette **❹⓪**.

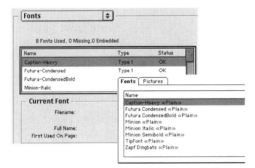

❸❾ The Font Usage dialog box is duplicated by the Fonts section of the Preflight dialog box.

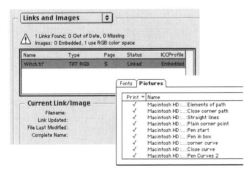

❹⓪ The Picture Usage dialog box is duplicated by the Links and Images section of the Preflight dialog box.

COMPARED TO PAGEMAKER 16

While there may be many people who will switch to InDesign from QuarkXPress, still many others will be coming from Adobe PageMaker. Adobe has worked hard to make PageMaker users feel comfortable switching over to InDesign. So PageMaker users will have an easy time making the transition to InDesign.

For intances, the Layers panel in InDesign is almost identical to the one in PageMaker. Many of the keyboard shortcuts from PageMaker have been incorporated into InDesign. However, there are some significant differences between PageMaker and InDesign.

This chapter will give you side-by-side comparisons of the two programs. After you read the material in this chapter, you can skip back to the previous chapters for more details.

TIP Each of the figures in this chapter displays the InDesign items on the left and the PageMaker items on the right.

Working with Tools

Most of the tools in PageMaker have direct counterparts in InDesign. The only big difference is found in the selection tools.

Selection Tools

- InDesign uses two selection tools to duplicate the functions of PageMaker's Selection tool ❶. *(See page 64.)*

- For graphics inside frames, InDesign's Direct Selection tool lets you move an object within the frame ❷. *(See page 121.)*

Rotation Tool

- InDesign's Rotation tool is very similar to PageMaker's Rotation tool ❸. The major difference is that you must first position the point of rotation in InDesign rather than just drag as in PageMaker. *(See page 66.)*

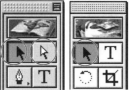

❶ The two InDesign selection tools duplicate PageMaker's Selection tool.

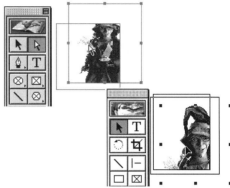

❷ The InDesign Direct Selection tool lets you move graphics inside frames. PageMaker's Selection tool moves the items inside masks.

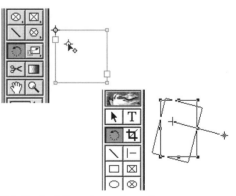

❸ InDesign's Rotation tool requires a two-step process, unlike PageMaker's simple drag.

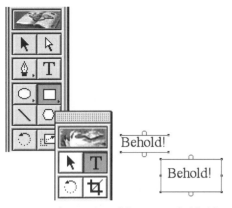

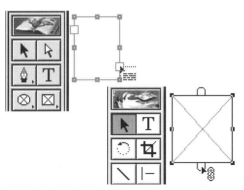

❹ InDesign's Unassigned frames can hold either text or graphics. This replaces PageMaker's windowshades or frames.

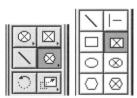

❺ InDesign's graphic frames are similar to PageMaker's frames.

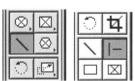

❻ InDesign's Line tool draws both angled and well as orthogonal lines.

❼ InDesign's Link box is located on the sides, not the top and bottom of frames.

Windowshades and Text Frames

- There are no specific windowshades for text in InDesign. Any frame can hold text or graphics **❹**. *(See page 60.)*

Graphic Frames

- The graphic frames are similar to the frames in PageMaker **❺**. *(See page 41.)*

Line Tools

- There is only one type of line tool in InDesign **❻**. Use the Shift key to constrain the lines to the orthogonal lines found in PageMaker. *(See page 61.)*

Text Link Tools

- InDesign's Link box is located on the sides, not the top and bottom, of frames **❼**. *(See page 56.)*

Working with Tools

Working with Boxes

There are a few differences in how you work
with boxes, or frames, in InDesign.

Box Shapes

- All frames in InDesign can be turned
  into other shapes by adding points with
  the Pen tool. There are no specific
  polygon, elliptical, or rectangular shapes
  in InDesign ❽.

- Unlike the closed frames in PageMaker,
  InDesign's frames do not have to be
  closed paths to hold text or graphics ❾.

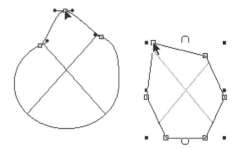

❽ InDesign lets you change the shape of any
frame with the Pen and selection tools.

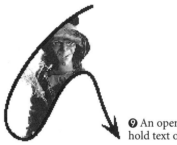

❾ An open frame can
hold text or a graphic.

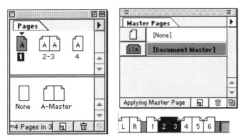

10 InDesign's Pages palette corresponds to PageMaker's pages controls and Master Pages palette.

Creating a Layout

There are some important differences in the document layout between PageMaker and InDesign.

Document Layout Palette

- InDesign's Pages palette corresponds to the pages controls and the Master Pages palette **10**. *(See page 134.)*

- InDesign's Pages palette also duplicates the features of PageMaker's Sort Pages dialog box **11**.

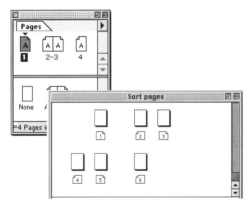

11 The Pages palette also duplicates the functions in PageMaker's Sort Pages dialog box.

Controlling Objects

InDesign's Transform palette duplicates many of the features of PageMaker's Control palette.

Text measurements palette

- Assemble the Transform and Character palettes together to duplicate PageMaker's Control palette for text objects ⓬.

- When the object is selected with the Selection tool, the Transform palette is visible.

- When the text is selected, the Character palette is visible.

- The character styles are found in the submenu of the Character palette ⓭.

Stroke palette

- InDesign's Stroke palette controls some of the features found in PageMaker's Stroke menu and Colors palette ⓮.

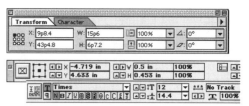

⓬ Use a combination of the Transform and Character palettes to duplicate the PageMaker Control palette for text boxes.

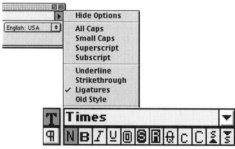

⓭ Use the Character palette submenu to apply character styles.

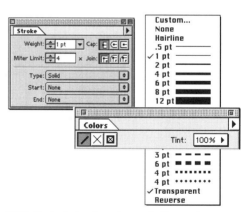

⓮ InDesign's Stroke palettes duplicates the features of the Colors palette and the Stroke menu.

Controlling Objects

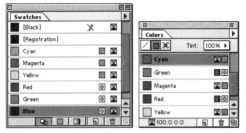

⓯ Use the InDesign Swatches palette as the equivalent of the PageMaker's Colors palette.

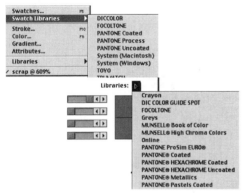

⓰ The color models, such as the Pantone colors, are found in the InDesign Swatches Libraries.

Creating Colors and Tints

Working with colors is very similar in the two programs.

Defining Colors

- PageMaker's Colors list is the equivalent of InDesign's Swatches palette **⓯**. *(See page 97.)*

TIP Try to avoid using InDesign's Color palette. This produces unnamed colors within the document that can cause problems later if you need to change those colors globally. *(See page 104.)*

Color Models

- Pantone colors and the other color models are found in InDesign's Swatches libraries **⓰**. *(See page 102.)*

Tints

- Tints of swatches can be made from the Color palette. They can then be applied to objects **⓱**. *(See page 103.)*

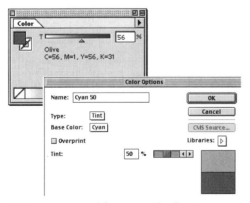

⓱ Tints are created from named colors in InDesign.

Creating Colors and Tints

Working with Text

Almost all of the text features in PageMaker are found in InDesign. However, they are located in different places.

Styles

- The PageMaker Styles palette is duplicated by InDesign's Paragraph Styles and Character Styles palettes **18**. *(See page 168.)*

Paragraph Rules

- The Paragraph Rules are found as part of the Paragraph Rules settings of the Paragraph palette submenu **19**. *(See page 189.)*

Word Spacing

- The Word Spacing settings are found as part of the Justification settings of the Paragraph palette submenu **20**. *(See page 182.)*

Display ¶

- There is no Story Editor in InDesign where you can display the paragraph symbols. However, you can display those symbols directly on the page. To show the paragraph symbols, choose **Type > Show Hidden Characters 21**. *(See page 55.)*

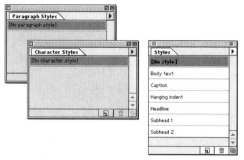

18 The Character Styles and Paragraph Styles palettes in InDesign duplicate PageMaker's Styles palette.

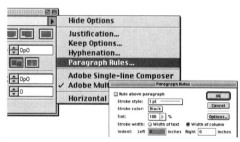

19 Paragraph Rules are found in the submenu of the Paragraph palette.

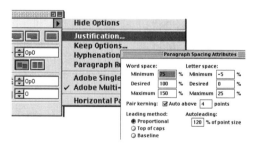

20 Spacing controls are found in the submenu of the Paragraph palette.

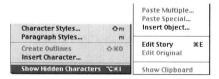

21 There is no Story Editor in InDesign. The Display ¶ command is duplicated by the Show Hidden Characters command.

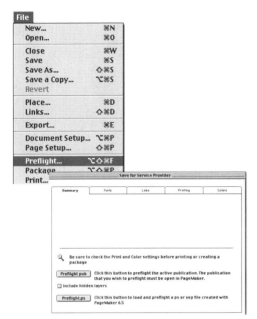

22 The features of the Prepare for Service Provider plug-in are contained in the Preflight and Package commands.

Outputting Files

While InDesign has many additional output options, there are some similarities to PageMaker.

Collect for Output

- The PageMaker Prepare for Service Provider plug-in appears as a combination of the Preflight and Package commands **22**. *(See pages 212 and 215.)*

Font Usage

- Document font usage is found as part of the Preflight package.

Picture Usage

- Link usage is found as part of the Preflight package and the Links palette.

INDEX

M

Index